SERGEI O. PROKOFIEFF, born in Moscow in 1954, studied painting and art history at the Moscow School of Art. He encountered anthroposophy in his youth, and soon made the decision to devote his life to it. He has been active as an author and lecturer since 1982, and in 1991 he co-founded the Anthroposophical Society in Russia. In Easter 2001 he became a member of the Executive Council of the General Anthroposophical Society in Dornach. This is his twentieth book to appear in English translation.

By the same author:

The Case of Valentin Tomberg
The Cycle of the Seasons and the Seven Liberal Arts
The Cycle of the Year as a Path of Initiation
The East in the Light of the West
The Encounter with Evil and its Overcoming through Spiritual Science
The Esoteric Significance of Spiritual Work in Anthroposophical Groups
Eternal Individuality, Towards a Karmic Biography of Novalis
The Foundation Stone Meditation
The Heavenly Sophia and the Living Being Anthroposophia
May Human Beings Hear It!
The Mystery of John the Baptist and John the Evangelist
The Occult Significance of Forgiveness
Prophecy of the Russian Epic
Rudolf Steiner and the Founding of the New Mysteries
Rudolf Steiner's Research into Karma and the Mission of the Anthroposophical Society
The Spiritual Origins of Eastern Europe and the Future Mysteries of the Holy Grail
The Twelve Holy Nights and the Spiritual Hierarchies
Valentin Tomberg, Rudolf Steiner and Anthroposophy
What is Anthroposophy?

Relating to Rudolf Steiner

and

The Mystery of the Laying of the Foundation Stone

SERGEI O. PROKOFIEFF

TEMPLE LODGE

Translated from German by Peggy Elliott

Temple Lodge Publishing
Hillside House, The Square
Forest Row, RH18 5ES

www.templelodge.com

Published by Temple Lodge 2008

© Sergei O. Prokofieff
This translation © Temple Lodge Publishing 2008

First published in German under the title *Von der Beziehung zu Rudolf Steiner* by Verlag am Goetheanum, Dornach, in 2006

The moral right of the author has been asserted under the Copyright, Designs and Patents Act, 1988

All rights reserved. No part of this publication may be reproduced, stored in a retrieval system, or transmitted, in any form or by any means, electronic, mechanical, photocopying or otherwise, without the prior permission of the publishers

A catalogue record for this book is available from the British Library

ISBN 978 1902636 95 5

Cover by Andrew Morgan
Typeset by DP Photosetting, Neath, West Glamorgan
Printed and bound by Cromwell Press Limited, Trowbridge, Wiltshire

Contents

Foreword   1

PART I: Relating to Rudolf Steiner
1. Trust Born of Freedom   5
2. Three Paths to Anthroposophy   12
3. The Mystery Surrounding Rudolf Steiner's Birthplace   18
4. A Path to Rudolf Steiner   31
5. Rudolf Steiner and the Founding Executive Council   43

PART II: The Mystery of the Laying of the Foundation Stone
1. Laying the Foundation Stone in 1923 as a Mystery Event   59
2. The New Community   66
3. The Spirit of the Goetheanum   74
4. Working with the New Group Souls   84
5. The Christmas Foundation Meeting and the Mystery of the Resurrection   97

APPENDIX:
1. The Esoteric Background to Electronic Media   101
2. Rudolf Steiner on the Youth of the Future   121

Notes   123
Sources of texts   137

Foreword

The following essays, slightly extended and published together for the first time in this compilation, were previously published in *Das Goetheanum* and in *Anthroposophie, Mitteilungen aus der anthroposophischen Arbeit in Deutschland* [German anthroposophical newsletter]. They were originally given as lectures at various locations.

Part 1 of this publication is in response to observations over recent years that a real relationship with Rudolf Steiner, even amongst our own supporters, is both weakening and becoming more problematic. Great efforts are needed to counter this, by striving for a closer connection. This is particularly necessary as support and encouragement for anthroposophists who realize that our whole future—not just that of the Anthroposophical Society but also of the anthroposophical movement—depends on whether a sufficient number of people can seek and find a real spiritual connection with Rudolf Steiner.

Although initial publication of some of these essays met with contrasting responses—understandable given the occult background of the subject itself—I have nevertheless decided to publish them together as a book, since I personally believe that the question of our relationship with Rudolf Steiner is fundamental to the life of anthroposophy itself.

At the Christmas Foundation Meeting Rudolf Steiner ensured that such a relationship with him would not remain merely general, abstract or intellectual but would become a real inner deed. By creating the spiritual Foundation Stone of the Anthroposophical Society he gave all of us the possibility to connect with this, his most important deed, through free inner work on the Foundation Stone. This is why he said at the end of the Christmas Foundation Meeting: '*We* have laid the Foundation Stone'—thus including in this event all anthroposophists who wish to follow the path of the new Mysteries.

This gives rise to a direct link between parts I and II of the book. Once a relationship with Rudolf Steiner is established, an inner longing to work with the new Mysteries inevitably follows. In other words, the *will* to take the foundation of the new Mysteries seriously is what, above all, leads to a real, inner connection with Rudolf Steiner.

Part II of this book describes some results of inner work with the Foundation Stone and the tasks arising from it for the Anthroposophical Society.

The two main parts of this book are supplemented by an appendix, part 1 of which which examines the problems underlying the recent electronic publication of Rudolf Steiner's most important esoteric texts. I have extended this text significantly in response to readers' questions about how one can counteract the damaging consequences of this development.

I think it is right to include this article in the present collection since our inner relationship with Rudolf Steiner, and spiritual work on the Foundation Stone, are an important aspect of what is needed to counteract such things.

Sergei O. Prokofieff
Goetheanum, Dornach, Easter 2006

PART I

Relating to Rudolf Steiner

1. Trust Born of Freedom

> *Freedom consists not in refusing*
> *to recognize anything higher than us,*
> *but in respecting what is higher than us;*
> *for, by respecting it, we raise ourselves to it,*
> *and, by our very acknowledgement, prove*
> *that we bear within ourselves what is higher,*
> *and are worthy to be on a level with it.*
> Goethe[1]

A necessary diagnosis

To seek ways into the future and away from the worrying situation in which the Anthroposophical Society, and increasingly the anthroposophical movement, find themselves today, one really almost needs the objectivity of medical science. If we first grasp the symptoms of the 'disease' we can then come to the right diagnosis. In doing so we may find that anthroposophy is not outmoded, and Rudolf Steiner still less so, but the real reason for the illness rests with us anthroposophists throughout the world.

A free creator of his age

Self-knowledge has always been, and still is, a difficult endeavour. We are constantly tempted to look for the reasons for our weaknesses and imperfections in others or elsewhere, instead of within ourselves. From long experience I can confirm that whenever one speaks or writes about core anthroposophical topics, real interest is shown both by anthroposophists and the wider public. Thus anthroposophy is still topical and vibrant today. Rudolf Steiner was someone who lived and worked with the new spiritual capacities which humanity will only come to develop in a distant future.

But what does it mean to be modern and topical? Lately it has repeatedly been said within anthroposophical circles that Rudolf

Steiner was 'a child of his time'. I wish to vehemently refute this. Childhood alone is the time for being a child. Only then is it right to be dependent on and influenced by parents and countless other circumstances relating to our surroundings. If we remain a dependent 'child' into adulthood then not only have we fallen outside normal, healthy human development but also outside the norm for the whole of humanity's development—and thus also for the age in which we live. Such a person could not therefore be called a 'child' of his time.

Rudolf Steiner, in contrast, was no 'child' of his time but the great human friend of the time spirit. Because of this was he able to speak, as only a close friend can, about the cosmic Michael Mystery of our era, the spiritual path and the inner world of this high hierarchical being. As such Rudolf Steiner was a collaborator with and indeed a 'real creator' of his age and the future.

In the penultimate chapter of his book *Knowledge of the Higher Worlds*, Rudolf Steiner describes how the student of spiritual science emancipates himself from all guidance of spiritual beings after his encounter with the lesser Guardian of the Threshold. From then on no group spirits lead him, not even the time spirit. This means that already at this level (which is not particularly advanced) he stops being a 'child'. This is what the modern path of initiation involves. From this level onwards the initiate has to create this relationship anew, freely, through the inner strength of his ego. By this means he gradually becomes a conscious colleague of the time spirit and a free creator within his epoch.

He who is free lives in trust

As Rudolf Steiner's pupils we can hardly be called friends of the time spirit since we are still predominantly children of our time. But Michael, whom Rudolf Steiner called the 'spiritual hero of freedom'[2] does not want to have 'children'. Our civilization today, however, lives under the sign of the anti-Michaelic zeitgeist which makes us dependent and impressionable. Therefore we still cannot deal with the many problems of the Anthroposophical Society as we succumb too often to the temptation to consciously or unconsciously accommodate or submit to the anti-spirit of our civilization rather than to be Michael's colleague.

In his book *The Philosophy of Freedom* Rudolf Steiner writes about the community of free human beings: 'It is only because human individuals *are* one in spirit that they can live out their lives side by side. The free person lives in confidence that he and any other free human beings belong to one spiritual world, and that their intentions will meet.'[3] In other words: Rudolf Steiner trusted us implicitly when he gave us his anthroposophy, in the hope that on the anthroposophical path of schooling we would freely raise ourselves up to the spiritual world of which he spoke, and out of which he worked, so that our intentions would meet with his intentions and thus with him.

Instead, some of his 'anthroposophical' critics go as far as regarding their criticism of Rudolf Steiner as an achievement of their own 'intuitive thinking'. In fact, on closer examination, this turns out to be merely ordinary, abstract intellectualism, which leads them to look for alleged mistakes, contradictions and dependencies in Rudolf Steiner rather than in themselves. True intuitive thinking is a wholly creative act that awakens and stimulates the capacity for moral imagination. In Rudolf Steiner this is clearly in evidence as can be seen from the fruits of anthroposophy. This however demands, at least imaginatively, some contact with the spiritual world which was the source of Rudolf Steiner's creative activity.

Rudolf Steiner—the first public initiate

This leads to further questions: What does it mean today to have a relationship with Rudolf Steiner? How can this relationship be nurtured and, especially, how can it be strengthened so that it becomes a steadfast basis for our work both within and outside the Anthroposophical Society?

Here I would like to make a personal remark. When I came to anthroposophy in the 1970s, Rudolf Steiner's great, innovative ideas in practical fields such as education, art, medicine and agriculture were for me not the most important thing. These 'only' put him alongside many other distinguished individuals of the 19th and 20th centuries. Of course I acknowledged his achievements with great awe and respect but that was not what really led me to Rudolf Steiner. For me the decisive fact was that for the first time in world history Rudolf Steiner, as an initiate of great spiritual significance, was able to work publicly amongst humanity. This was also someone whose initiation was founded on the newest faculties of our time, the ability to explore and describe the spiritual world with the same exact clarity as a natural scientist.

At the same time I immediately realized that Rudolf Steiner, as an initiate, could not fit into any of our contemporary categories because modern culture does not recognize initiates. It accommodates scientists, artists, doctors, researchers and explorers but there is no place in public life for an initiate.

Today, therefore, we can only find our way to Rudolf Steiner as pupils. This means following him in earnest effort on the path he took before us, and described in detail. We also constantly have to remind ourselves that we follow in the footsteps of Rudolf Steiner with the aim of eventually entering a spiritual world where free collaboration with him will be possible.

The path of devotion

How does the anthroposophical path of schooling lead to modern initiation? What are the basic conditions? Rudolf Steiner describes this at the beginning of the first chapter of *Knowledge of the Higher Worlds,* his primary text on personal development. In the very first pages he speaks of the 'basic mood' needed for the whole of the path, which he calls a 'path of initiation'. For modern initiation this mood has to be practised in all its aspects including the following: 'If I meet someone and blame him for his shortcomings, I rob myself of the power to attain higher knowledge; but if I try to enter lovingly into his merits, I gather such power.'[4] This law applies irrevocably at all levels, which is why Rudolf Steiner emphasizes it so strongly, at the same time pointing out that this quality in particular is lacking in modern civilization. This is also why our culture does not offer a good basis for higher development.

Of course we also have to voice criticism in certain situations—but every time one resorts to it, or believes one has to, one deprives oneself of forces of knowledge in a quite objective sense. In response to a question about how this affected people such as newspaper critics whose profession involves continual criticism, Rudolf Steiner once said: 'They have the least favourable karma for spiritual development.'[5]

In our times in particular the capacity for devotion is of central significance as the most important teacher of the consciousness soul.[6] Thus we could regard it as a consciousness soul exercise to apply the above-mentioned rule in relation to Rudolf Steiner and to 'lovingly immerse ourselves in the benefits gained from him'. If we can really do this we will never again feel obliged to probe for supposed errors, and the theoretical question of whether mistakes can be found in Rudolf Steiner's work also becomes completely irrelevant.

This does not, of course, negate the fact that certain passages in his work may raise questions for the pupil, which he is unable to answer or resolve immediately. But it will also repeatedly happen, sometimes even after years, that this very difficulty or apparently contradictory passage suddenly reveals its secret and becomes a stepping-stone for unexpected spiritual perspectives and horizons of knowledge. One just needs to be patient and live with an unanswered question for a while rather than forming a hasty or premature judgement.

By this means, and by studying his work, we can gradually approach Rudolf Steiner over time. In this context he writes: 'Regard a book such as this as a conversation which the author has with the reader.'[7] This experience can grow even stronger when studying his lectures. The moment one experiences this kind of inner conversation with the spiritual teacher, all talk of the 'incomprehensibility' of anthroposophical content, or of Rudolf Steiner's 'difficult' language—not to mention doubt about the value of such study itself—appears futile. Without study, and a great deal of study, there is no way to meet Rudolf Steiner on the path of schooling. Study is the anthroposophical foundation for the entire schooling path: conversation with the teacher through such study can lead to a spiritual encounter via meditative practice.

A connection that reaches into the spiritual world

The anthroposophical path of schooling, which Rudolf Steiner also calls the modern Rosicrucian path of initiation, and which he says is the sole path compatible with humanity's development in the West, involves a wholly new kind of relationship with one's spiritual teacher. On the old, oriental path, spiritual development was not possible 'without strong submission to the authority of the guru'; and on the so-called 'Christian gnostic path', too, constant monitoring by the teacher, who had to be physically present, was an important condition. On the modern Rosicrucian schooling path a completely new relationship exists, rooted in real friendship between teacher and pupil. Here the authority of the spiritual teacher rests solely on its free acceptance by the pupil. In other words, such authority is founded on freely gained and given trust. The physical presence of the teacher is no longer necessary. Even when the teacher is long dead, therefore, he can guide his pupils from the spiritual world, and still retain their complete trust as the fundamental condition of pupilship.

The words with which Rudolf Steiner described the modern Rosicrucian path make clear what emphasis he placed on this condition:

> With the Rosicrucian way the guru becomes more and more a friend whose authority is based on inner assent. The only possible relationship in this case is one of complete personal trust. The least bit of distrust between teacher and pupil would break the bond that has to exist between them, and then the powers that come into play between teacher and pupil would no longer be effective.[8]

That Rudolf Steiner wished to build the whole esoteric relationship with his pupils on this basis of trust was clear not only at the beginning of his work as spiritual teacher, but right up to the end of his life—for example in his lecture of 30 January 1924, where he also emphasizes the importance of this trust for the existence of the School of Spiritual Science.[9] He was not just referring, here, to trust in him and in what he gave as the School of Spiritual Science, but also to trust amongst his pupils.

This brings us to an essential point of this book. Ita Wegman's words about the dangers of 'ahrimanization' of anthroposophy should it become separated from Rudolf Steiner in the world,[10] mean, firstly, that when an anthroposophist applies what he has gained through Rudolf Steiner's spiritual teachings he should also quote his name as his source (this is one of the most elementary proprieties in the scientific world). However I also believe that the words of Steiner which Ita Wegman here repeats, relate primarily to the inner and true spiritual relationship between his pupils and Rudolf Steiner himself. If this inner relationship to him is missing then such a representation of anthroposophy is subject to the diluting effect referred to, which is thus exactly 'what ahrimanic beings want and aim for'.[11]

The relationship with Rudolf Steiner

Nowadays it is possible to have a merely distant, historical relationship to Rudolf Steiner in the same way as one might have to any other important personality of the past, such as Mozart or Goethe. Alternatively, we can choose to look to Rudolf Steiner as our personal spiritual teacher who still guides his pupils from the spiritual world, and who can talk to them in the depths of their souls.

It is no secret that this kind of intimate relationship with Rudolf Steiner meets with resistance and increasing rejection even from anthroposophists. And yet everyone who sincerely adopts this inner path of relationship with Rudolf Steiner and pursues it to a sufficient extent, will be able to testify from his own experience about moments of elevation and enlightenment. For such people, these encounters with Rudolf Steiner's spiritual presence count amongst the highest and happiest moments in their life.

In *The Philosophy of Freedom* Rudolf Steiner writes: 'The free person does not demand agreement from his fellow human beings, but expects to find it because it is inherent in human nature.'[12] Thus was Rudolf Steiner's relationship to trust. He never asked for it but expected this trust because it is inherent in human nature, which means it lies within those human forces which are the sole basis for the modern path of schooling.

Only if such trust in its founder is heartfelt among the members of the Anthroposophical Society, and if members of the School of Spiritual Science also make it their central concern, can the Anthroposophical Society count on Rudolf Steiner's help and involvement with its work in the world. Without this, furthermore, it will never be able to fulfil the spiritual and human task with which it has been entrusted.

2. Three Paths to Anthroposophy

A new kind of devotion

Contradictions, which the abstract intellect believes exist within anthroposophy, in fact ask for a new quality of thinking—one capable of creating independent connections out of its own activity, by means of which these supposed contradictions are then transformed into a path of knowledge. In Rudolf Steiner's book *Knowledge of the Higher Worlds* one reads about three stages in which the necessary condition of devotion can be developed, but which may appear to conflict with the ordinary intellect.

The first stage is a childlike devotion. Here the child adores a specific person and, as is justified at this age, has a certain dependency on them since a child imitates. At a certain age, this ability to imitate is a quality that aids development. In fact, this first stage is an absolutely necessary precondition for moving on to a second stage in later life, that of 'devotion to truth and knowledge'. If this is practised correctly then one can ascend to the third stage, that of appreciation and devotion towards a certain person, but now out of complete inner freedom and without any dependency. This implies a wholly new kind of devotion, one born from a deep recognition of this person and their highest aims, and based on the understanding that for great, advanced individualities, who not only speak about the truth but also live and embody it, such truth gradually becomes part of their innermost being and can no longer be separated from them. This does not in the least negate human freedom.

The highest ideal of truth

In this respect, Christ Jesus represents the highest embodiment of the ideal of supreme truth, which is why He could say: 'I am the Truth' (St John 14, 6). This reflects the transition from a still imperfect and limited relationship to truth as content to a higher relationship to truth as being. It also points to the path which every real Christian initiate treads, including Rudolf Steiner. His whole life's work is based on research into the spiritual world, the world of truth. This world of truth does not consist of abstract concepts but of different kinds of spiritual beings who themselves manifest different levels of truth. Thus, throughout his life, Rudolf Steiner could reveal the spiritual world in a modern scientific guise in his writing and speech only because his being embodied some of this truth. We can surely honour this fact with devotion born of freedom—a devotion rooted in real human understanding.

Rudolf Steiner was able to express such devotion in his due acknowledgement of other great masters of humanity. He often conveyed this, in particular in his 'esoteric lessons': 'I am able and allowed to be your leader only insofar as the exalted Master by whom *I myself am guided* gives me instructions.'[13] 'And, for the moment, I greet you therewith in the name of the holy Master at whose feet I lay all that I have, and against whose will I shall never knowingly transgress during life. Blessed be they, the exalted ones.[14]

Friedrich Rittelmeyer likewise remembers a conversation with Rudolf Steiner about his spiritual teacher:

> Nor shall I ever forget the expression on his face when he said of one of these two men: 'That was a most significant personality.' His eyes seemed to be steeped in contemplation of him. They were filled with the reverence paid by one great knower to another.'[15]

With these words Rudolf Steiner did not suddenly assume an old-fashioned 'theosophical' habit or negate his high ideals as expressed in *The Philosophy of Freedom*. This involves serious occult laws, which cannot be judged simply by a 'philistine' standard of 'just wanting to feel free'.

Obviously such inner trust, which alone creates the basis for true devotion, is not achieved immediately. First it has to be developed out of freedom and knowledge. But once this trust and devotion has been established it is no longer 'blind trust' or 'naïve devotion' as in 'traditional piety'; in fact it has nothing at all to do with old forces of this kind. Rudolf Steiner does not of course reject all justified veneration of a genius or other exceptionally gifted person—as is clear from his words in *Knowledge of the Higher Worlds:* 'We can sincerely revere these favoured of God; but we should not for this reason regard the work of esoteric training as superfluous.'

It is wrong to simply quote Rudolf Steiner's words—'I don't wish to be revered but understood'—as counter-argument, precisely because this new kind of devotion does not *precede* true understanding of the other but, in contrast, *results* and actually arises from it.

Criticism and naivety

In recent years it has become increasingly noticeable that some anthroposophists, who can be grateful to Rudolf Steiner for his insights and who fundamentally owe him everything, voice criticism which even reaches the level of censure. Frequently such criticism is carried into the wider public arena. I don't believe that such criticism is simply based on questions that might have arisen from the study of Rudolf Steiner's work, because a fully developed consciousness soul will take this as a challenge.

In my opinion this criticism by some anthroposophists of Rudolf Steiner is not an accomplishment of the consciousness soul and certainly not the fruit of highly developed intuitive thinking but more likely the result of unrecognized naivety. Why?

In the cycle *Human and Cosmic Thought*[16] Rudolf Steiner presents the truth as being a harmony between twelve different points of view or, indeed, twelve world views.[17] This insight gives us a vital methodological approach for anthroposophy. The spiritual world is in reality highly complex, and cannot easily be understood with earthly concepts because of its fundamental difference from the physical world. A spiritual researcher therefore has to consider the same spiritual phenomena repeatedly from different points of view in order to clarify them.

If one takes photographs of a tree from different angles and compares them with each other, an ordinary person might conclude that, because the photos all look different, each one depicts a different tree or that the pictures contradict each other. Rudolf Steiner relates this example to spiritual truths. Of course, for ordinary intellectual understanding the photographs may be contradictory, and this can only be overcome through active, coherent thinking. Thus Rudolf

Steiner tried to show that the arguments of 19th-century rational theology—which struggled with apparent contradictions in the four Gospels—were incorrect because in reality the Gospels represent four different, archetypal and mutually complementary points of view of the same truth.

You may notice that we are here addressing a higher level of connection with Rudolf Steiner where no 'doubt' of any kind is justified. Here we are no longer concerned with the stage of study but with a further one which simply cannot be achieved without a deep connection between spiritual pupil and spiritual teacher. Once it has been attained, however, by embracing the path of schooling with steadfast perseverance, it will continue beyond death.

Doubt too has different consequences on the various stages of the path of schooling. Whilst doubt may be valuable at the outset, when we begin to study spiritual science it not only becomes a hindrance later on but can grow to be one of the greatest enemies of higher knowledge. Yet we will only be able to acknowledge this through enlivened thinking, which does not create contradictions but clearly recognizes that the same soul qualities at different stages of development can have different, even polar opposite connotations. By failing to recognize this, one remains unwittingly within 'naive perception'.

So whether one can be an anthroposophist without regarding oneself as Rudolf Steiner's pupil depends on what we understand by 'being an anthroposophist'. As far as this concerns someone who wishes to go no further than forming an acquaintance with anthroposophy through study, the answer is yes. However, if one wishes to become a true spiritual pupil along the lines indicated in the book *Knowledge of the Higher Worlds,* then Rudolf Steiner himself gives the answer: Here personal trust in the spiritual teacher is indispensable. Otherwise this path simply cannot be pursued. This sentiment can be found in many of Rudolf Steiner's works.[18]

Three paths to anthroposophy

In his essay *Theosophie und gegenwärtige Geistesströmungen* ('Theosophy and contemporary spiritual streams') Rudolf Steiner describes three paths which can today lead people to anthroposophy and thus to the reality of the supersensible world.[19] The first path is based on a 'healthy and natural feeling for the truth' as contained in insights given by the spiritual researcher. This 'feeling for the truth', however, is a quality increasingly disappearing from modern civilization. However, this path is of special importance. Rudolf Steiner writes:

> They [who take this path] allow their feeling to be permeated with what theosophy [anthroposophy] presents, and this feeling, unclouded by philosophy and scientific criticism, tells them that what they encounter there is true.... Those who thus become followers of theosophy [anthroposophy] are in a certain sense the most important, the most valuable.

Here Rudolf Steiner also emphasizes the sense of trust.

It is quite clear that he does not see this first path as less important than the other two. He even accords it special importance, and continues: 'Someone whose healthy feeling has not been spoiled by intellectualized understanding really perceives the truth.'

The second path, which Rudolf Steiner describes in his book *Knowledge of the Higher Worlds,* leads directly to the spiritual world. But a requirement of this path particularly is that when choosing to become a spiritual pupil we show complete trust in the guide who leads us. In our case this means trust in Rudolf Steiner. Thus we find in the same essay:[20] 'For the seeker no other means are available than the trust he can have in the person from whom he receives such guidance.' The essay also speaks of 'ever greater, unshakeable faith in spiritual knowledge'.

The third path is one suitable for a person 'soundly schooled in philosophy', who has acquired a 'deep knowledge of philosophy—not one that has stopped half way'. The source of such a 'sound philosophy' is found in the great thinkers of German Idealism as well as in Rudolf Steiner's early philosophical works. However, we should not confuse this 'philosophical path' with the philosophical persuasion of the Sceptics, whose best-known representative was Michel de Montaigne. His famous saying: 'To philosophize means to doubt' does not lead us further on this third path; but we need, rather, a completely different inner attitude. This can be found particularly in the philosophy of Fichte, Schelling and Hegel, who were not concerned with 'doubt' of whatever kind but, on the contrary, with unshakeable trust in the power of human thinking, and thus in the human being himself.

★

Having worked seriously with anthroposophy for thirty years I am convinced that in Rudolf Steiner we find one of the truest, purest and most beautiful human spirits that ever lived on earth. His biography too is a mystery which has not yet been fully explored.

For me Rudolf Steiner is, more than almost anyone else, a modern witness to Christ in that he not only spoke and wrote about spiritual realities but also lived and embodied them with his whole being.

Our devotion to Rudolf Steiner increases the more we understand him, and is objectively rooted in the path of schooling which he gave us. Such devotion does not arise in a healthy human soul because Rudolf Steiner demands it, but is born in complete freedom as a totally new capacity of the future, which we can only nurture in the way expressed in Goethe's words at the beginning of chapter 1.

3. The Mystery Surrounding Rudolf Steiner's Birthplace

Place of birth

In a private conversation, Rudolf Steiner once spoke about the future reincarnation of Mani, the founder of Manichaeism, in the 21st century. Mani was incarnated as the Grail king Parsifal in the 9th century. 'Mani will not re-incarnate in this century,' said Steiner, 'he intends to do that in the following century if he can find a suitable body.'[21] And he added that it would be an important task of Waldorf education to make possible the reincarnation of highly developed spirits: 'Ordinary education does not offer a developmental possibility for Mani; only Waldorf education does so.'[22] In the light of this we can assume that the question of opportunities for reincarnation also affected Rudolf Steiner himself. The following attempts to shed some light on the circumstances of his birth.

Rudolf Steiner was born on 25 February 1861 in the village of Kraljevec (which means 'seat of kings'), part of modern Croatia. On 27 February he was baptized under the name of Rudolf Joseph Lorenz at the Catholic Church in the neighbouring village of Drakovec. The region then belonged to Hungary but was mainly populated by Croats so that the language the boy mostly heard besides German was Slovak.

His parents came from Central Austria. Both were born in the wooded region of Lower Austria, north of the Danube. His father, Johannes Steiner, came from Geras, and his mother, Franziska, née Blie, from Horn. Johannes Steiner moved from Geras to Horn to work as gamekeeper for the Count of Hoyos. Whilst still in his hometown he frequently mixed with very educated monks of the Prämonstratenser order. From them he learned the importance of education, and longed to educate his future children.

When Johannes Steiner wanted to marry Franziska Blie, whom he had met during his time in service, the Count refused his request. Consequently the freedom-loving Johannes Steiner handed in his notice, trained as stationmaster with the Southern Austrian Railway, and left the region with his young wife.

At first Johannes Steiner was sent to a station whose name has been lost, but it was somewhere in Southern Styria (probably between Marburg an der Drau [today's Maribor] and Laibach [today's Ljubljana]). That was in the summer of 1860.[23] Shortly before Rudolf Steiner's birth, around January 1861, the railway's management moved his father to Kraljevec. There Rudolf Steiner was born as the first of three children. (His sister Leopoldine, 1864–1927, and brother Gustav 1866–1941, were both born in Pottschach.) It is not insignificant that his parents not only lived in this special region of Europe at the time of his birth but also already while his mother was pregnant with him.

Due to these circumstances Rudolf Steiner was born far away from his parents' homeland, amongst foreigners. From the beginning of his life a pattern of rootlessness is apparent, something which today, in the era when the consciousness soul is developing, plays a part in many people's lives.

In a lecture for Russians, which Rudolf Steiner gave on 11 April 1912 in Helsinki, he referred to these circumstances in the following words: 'Those who were the bearers ... of the blood from which I descend, came from German areas of Austria—where I was not born. I myself was born in a Slavic region, one wholly foreign to the familiar environment and customs of my forefathers.'[24]

At birth the child was very delicate and weak and was not expected to live very long. It was therefore thought important to have him baptized, despite the cold, wintry weather. Because the midwife had swaddled the newborn child badly, bleeding occurred which was not immediately noticed. For many hours the child bled until his nappy turned red. Thus, loss of blood was one of his very first experiences.

Born on the border between the German and Slavic peoples who were then part of the Austro-Hungarian Empire—a border which simultaneously represented a spiritual-scientific boundary between the ego and spirit-self culture of the present and future—Rudolf Steiner was already embedded by this fact in the future task of anthroposophy: that of finding the way from the individual I to the spirit self, and thus to a new, conscious relationship with the spiritual world. Only in the free I of the human being can the inner fire kindle that enables us to develop spiritually from below upwards. Through the spirit self in contrast, guided by the element of light, the spiritual revelation flows from above downwards. Rudolf Steiner later spoke of his spiritual research and spiritual revelations as the two sources of anthroposophy.

He therefore owed the forces of ego development to his Austrian descent, while light-born revelation of the spirit came to him from the etheric surroundings of his place of birth. Kraljevec lies on the so-called Isle of Mur, a peninsula narrowing towards the East, surrounded by the rivers Mur and Drau, which, after merging, flow into the Danube. The flat, sandy ground of this region makes nature specially receptive to the etheric properties of light. This peninsula extending below open skies is reminiscent of Mesopotamia, repeated here on a small scale albeit covered in ample vegetation and forest.

In addition to the Germanic and Slavic elements[25] there is a third, Celtic element, in this region. Thousands of years ago this area, as well as Styria in the North, was populated by Celts. Marie Steiner later wrote about Rudolf Steiner's roots: 'Germanness imbued with Slavonic culture rooted in Celtic tribal strength.'[26]

According to Rudolf Steiner's spiritual research, the archangel of the Celts fulfilled his task for Celtic culture particularly well, but did not then ascend to higher rank, instead sacrificing himself to remain as archangel. As such he continued to work as spiritual guide and inspiration for esoteric Christianity and in particular for the Mysteries of the Grail.[27] Thus it is not surprising that vital episodes relating to the Mystery of the Grail took place in the region where Rudolf Steiner was later born.

The Grail Mystery of the Isle of Mur

The contents of this chapter are largely based on Viktor Stracke's (Graz, Austria) commendable essay: 'Mystery places in old Austria. The Path of Trevrizent.'[28]

During his many and widespread walking tours, the great Grail Poet, Wolfram von Eschenbach, also came to Aquileia near the northern shores of the Adriatic. His benefactor, Wolfger von Leuprechtskirchen, Bishop of Passau from 1191 to 1204 and friend of Walther von der Vogelweide, later became patriarch of Aquileia. In his diocese the tradition of independent Irish-Scottish Christianity had been kept alive, and hence maintained a greater independence from Rome. Wolfram von Eschenbach was therefore able to visit his friend and patron in Aquileia without danger. It is probable that the first eight books of the Parsifal epic were written at that time. Much points to the fact that Wolfram wrote the next, ninth book in Aquileia or nearby. Consequently it contains a detailed description of this region, which stretches northeast from Aquileia to the Isle of Mur.[29]

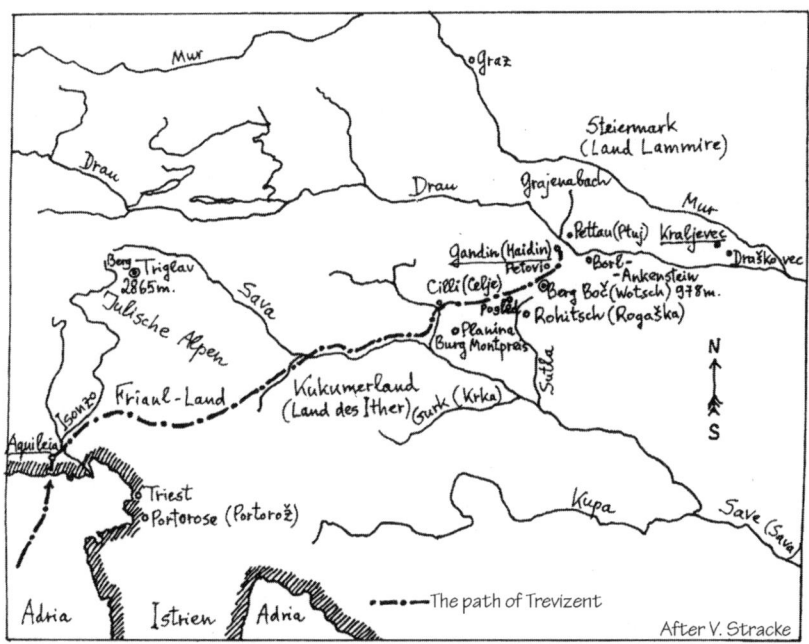

The ninth book describes Trevrizent's journey to his friend Gahmuret, the future father of Parsifal. They had planned this visit in Spanish Seville, and now Trevrizent travels by boat to Aquileia in order to continue from there by horse to Gahmuret's ancestral seat, accompanied by the young knight Ither. This ancestral seat was named Gandin after Gahmuret's father, who at that time also owned the region south of Styria.[30] (In chapter nine Wolfram mentions Styria, clearly identifying this region.)

Their ride leads them through the region of Frilau, northeast of Aquileia, then along the river Save to the town of Cilli, passing Mount Wotsch,[31] with the town of Rohitsch further towards the East, until they reach the place 'where the Grajena-Stream flows into the Drau' (*Parsifal*, book 9). This place, Gandin or Haidin, was situated on the southern shores of the Drau opposite the magnificent town and castle of Pettau (today Ptuj) north of the river, which still exists today.

South of the river, however, where at that time a Roman settlement was already located, Gahmuret's father Gandin's ancestral castle may have stood.[32] After his elder brother Galoes's death, Gahmuret became regent of this area including the Isle of Mur.[33] At that time Gahmuret had long left Gandin and lived in Castle Ankenstein (Borl), further down the river, east of Pettau. As was then customary, he had left his father's castle as a young man and moved to Ankenstein as his main residence—that is, he had it built. To his panther crest (which is still to be found in the Styrian crest) he added an anchor, reflecting the name of the castle.

During his many journeys Gahmuret meets the French Queen Anflise, probably through the mediation of an Arthurian knight, who presents him with a page, a little boy from the line of King Arthur, called Schionatulander.[34] Gahmuret and Herzeloide adopt the boy; he is brought up as their son and educated in all knightly skills. Later, not only as Gahmuret's page but also his closest friend, he accompanies him on all his journeys. Thus the young Schionatulander also has the difficult task, which however also specially bonds him with Gahmuret, of bringing the news of the latter's death in the Orient to his wife Herzeloide who is heavily pregnant with Parsifal.

Sigune too, Herzeloide's niece, lives from the age of five, after her mother's death during childbirth, in the castle with Gahmuret and Herzeloide. The two children grow up together and become very close. This is how Schionatulander comes into direct contact with representatives of the Grail, as both the Grail king, Amfortas, and also Trevrizent and Sigune's mother, are Herzeloide's siblings.

Schionatulander's special destiny links him not only with Parsifal's parents but also with the future Grail king himself. One day, as they sit in front of their tent, a dog with a beautiful collar bearing mysterious signs runs past Sigune and Schionatulander. Before Sigune is able to take a closer look the dog runs off. Now, Sigune is eager to read these signs and asks her page to find the dog with the precious collar. (It would go beyond the scope of this essay to enter into the occult meaning of this chapter and the signs on the collar.) During his search Schionatulander meets the knight Orals who, full of rage, is looking for Parsifal who has kissed Orilus's wife Jeschute completely innocently a short while before, and taken her ring and brooch. Now Orilus wants revenge and to kill Parsifal. In the forest, however, he meets Schionatulander and in his rage mistakes him for Parsifal and slays him.

In this way a very special karmic knot is tied between Schionatulander and the future Grail king. Because of his wrongdoing against Jeschute, Parsifal should have died with all the tragic consequences which would have arisen from this for the destiny of the Grail Mysteries on earth. Higher powers, however, allow someone else to sacrifice himself for Parsifal, and thus the future of the Grail Mysteries is saved. It can be said that Schionatulander unknowingly saves the future of esoteric Christianity for mankind by his premature death.

Because of this, the encounter between Sigune, with her dead fiancée on her lap, makes such an inexplicable impression on Parsifal. Before his eyes tears are being shed for the one who took his place in death. After this encounter Parsifal's spirit consciousness slowly awakens and his long and difficult path of initiation to become the Grail king begins.

To Viktor Stracke's research we can add the fact that, into the 20th century in the region around Mount Wotsch,[35] legends were circulating amongst the population that were reminiscent of Lohengrin. In accordance with what has been said this is entirely possible, as Lohengrin, Parsifal's son and Gandin's great nephew, might have retired to his ancestor's seat in order to be called from there by the Grail to the aid of Elsa von Brabant.

We know that after Lohengrin the Holy Grail was finally returned to the spiritual world in order to be cared for by the angels under the guardianship of the former archangel of the Celts. In his lecture of 23 July 1922, Rudolf Steiner mentions that specially chosen people, who during their lifetime were able to offer something unique in their service to the spiritual world, for a while become guardians of the Grail in the spiritual world after their death, alongside the angels. 'Specially chosen souls after death were appointed as guardians of the Holy Grail. One will never be completely able to understand the legend of the

Grail if one does not know who the guardians of the Grail actually were.'[36]

Thus Schionatulander was not only on intimate terms with many members of the Grail dynasty but, like Parsifal later, himself pursued the path from the Arthurian to the Grail knighthood and was inadvertently the saviour of the Mysteries of the Grail. After his sacrificial death he was therefore prepared to enter the circle of human guardians of the Grail in the spiritual world and to come into direct contact with the archangel of esoteric Christianity who later also became the inspiration for Rosicrucianism.[37]

During the Christmas Foundation Meeting[38] Rudolf Steiner pointed to the esoteric relationship between the Hibernian Mysteries rooted in Celtic tradition and the ensuing Mysteries of the Grail, and also the later Mysteries of the Rosicrucians, who in a new era became the spiritual successors of the Grail Stream.[39] This shows a consistent thread within the development of the Mysteries, which, as already mentioned, stood under the guidance and custody of the erstwhile Celtic archangel. And those human souls or 'living dead' were also effective as supersensible inspiration in these esoteric streams.

In the same lecture Rudolf Steiner mentions that Lohengrin belonged to the occult 'Knightly Order of the Swan', whose members, because of their special initiation, became the 'outer sheath' of the guardians of the Grail living in the spiritual world. Those who were dedicated to the 'Knightly Order of the Swan' wanted the knights of the Grail to work through them in the physical world in order to guide Europe's destiny.

The individuality Schionatulander also belongs to these guardians of the Grail who worked through the 'Knightly Order of the Swan' on earth. Therefore it is not surprising that legends similar to Lohengrin arose in the region where he spent his youth.

An important intermediate phase in Rudolf Steiner's karmic biography

In his lecture of 14 August 1924 Rudolf Steiner mentions, just once, that in the incarnations of Aristotle and his pupil Alexander—which he takes as theme of his karma lectures of 1924—there was an intermediate incarnation in the 9th century in the region of the Grail Mysteries.

> When they then brought their karma into earthly life ... they actually lived unnoticed, dying early in a corner of Europe that is, however, important for anthroposophy.... They only as it were gazed through a window into occidental civilization for a short period, gathering impressions and impulses but not themselves giving any kind of impetus—something which they had to reserve for later.[40]

From information which Rudolf Steiner gave Ita Wegman we can gather that this incarnation of Schionatulander was his own.[41] In addition to the conversations with Ita Wegman he also pointed out, in conversations with Elisa von Moltke and Walter Johannes Stein about the history of the Grail in the 9th century, that the encounter between Parsifal and Sigune, who lamented her dead fiancé, occurred in the region close to the Hermitage in Arlesheim. We may therefore presume that Schionatulander's death at the hands of Orilus also occurred here.

This leads to a wonderful connection between the places of Rudolf Steiner's birth and death. He was born in Kraljevec not far from where Schionatulander spent his youth and apprenticeship as Gahmuret's page.[42] He died on 30 March 1925, cared for and accompanied into death by his doctor friend, in Dornach, close to Arlesheim, in direct proximity to the place where Schionatulander was killed in the 9th century, and lamented and buried by Sigune.

This also explains why in Rudolf Steiner's karmic biography this short intermediate incarnation in the 9th century was of such crucial importance for the later founding of anthroposophy as a 'Science of the Grail' (*Occult Science*). In order for karmic relationships to bear fruit after death, they have to be established on earth. This is particularly true of Schionatulander's numerous connections with those who stood closest to the Mysteries of the Grail in the 9th century. And as this karmic knot was tied even closer by his sacrificial death for Parsifal, Schionatulander's soul was able to build on this connection in the supersensible world. It is possible that this soul was the one who accompanied and inspired Parsifal from the spiritual world on his long path of trials to become the Grail king. If so, then the individuality of Schionatulander would also have been present at the initiation of Parsifal—which Rudolf Steiner calls 'the ideal of the new initiation' insofar as it depends on the consciousness soul.[43] After his death this brought Schionatulander into direct contact with the archangel of esoteric Christianity and into the circle of supersensible guardians of the Grail, and later made him into a significant representative of true Rosicrucianism.

In the 20th century, therefore, Rudolf Steiner was able to outline a modern 'Science of the Grail' in his book *Occult Science* and offer Parsifal's path of initiation in an appropriately modern form to all people of good will. The path into the supersensible worlds outlined as first steps in that book leads to the 'Science of the Grail'.

Rudolf Steiner, as leading initiate of the Grail, did not stop there. Once he had completed his book he went much further in revealing the Mysteries of the Grail.

Within the forms of the first Goetheanum, as a modern Grail castle on earth, he was able to make the 'Science of the Grail' visible to all and later, at the Christmas Foundation Meeting, he gave humanity the being of the Grail itself to care for and guard, in the form of the Foundation Stone.[44]

In doing so Rudolf Steiner revealed his mission in the Mysteries of the Grail, and his true Mystery name as the Guardian of the Grail in our time.[45]

Out of his deep connection with the archangel of esoteric Christianity Rudolf Steiner was able to renew true Rosicrucianism on earth and inseparably link it with the Mysteries of the Grail. This is borne out by the fact that in *Occult Science* he also characterizes the seven-stage Rosicrucian initiation as Grail initiation, and calls himself, and those who undertake this path today, initiates of the Grail.[46]

Rudolf Steiner thus pointed to his central position within esoteric Christianity, and we find the karmic roots for this in his short incarnation in the 9th century and its consequences after death.

Wolfram von Eschenbach's narrative

Finally let us quote the relevant texts by Wolfram von Eschenbach himself. They belong to the few places in *Parsifal* where geographical names are very precise, because Wolfram came to know the region very well as he walked or travelled through it.

Wolfram has Trevrizent describe his journey as follows:

And once, when my adventures had led me to the Rohas,
a valiant host of Wends came out to offer me combat.
From Seville I had sailed all round the sea to Aquileia, then to Cilli by way of Friuli.
O alas and alas, that ever I saw your father; it was then I came to know him, when I arrived in Seville. The noble Angevin had taken lodgings there before me.

He also gave his kinsman as squire,
Ither, the King of Kukumerlant, whose heart was so true it knew no falsehood.
But we did not want to delay our journeys longer and we went our separate ways.
He returned to the Baruch, and I rode to the Rohas.

Riding out from Cilli I came to the Rohas,
and for three Mondays I fought hard and, I thought, very well. From there I rode with all speed to vast Gandine,
from which your grandfather Gandin had his name.
And there Ither was well known.
That city lies just where the Grajena flows into the Drau,
a stream that has gold in it. And there Ither was loved.
Your father's sister was queen of that land, and he saw her now again.
Gandin of Anjou had made her the ruler there. Lammire is her name, and the kingdom is called Styria. He who follows the service
of the shield must range through many lands![47]

In this excerpt all geographic names can be directly linked to places still in existence today.

- *Rohas* is now Rohasberg or Rohitschberg, also called Mount Wotsch
- *Cilli* in Slovak is Celje (in antiquity Celeia)
- *Aquileia*, a former port in antiquity at the most northern shores of the Adriatic; today only ruins are left

- *Friuli* lies north east of Aquileia and south of the Julian Alps
- *Kukumerlant* lies east of Friuli between the rivers Save (Sava) in the north and Gurk (Krka) in the south
- *Gandien* or Hajdin, a suburb of Pettau (today Ptuj, in antiquity Petovio), lies on the right shore of the river Drau, opposite the hill with the castle
- the stream *Grajena*, which flows into the Drau at the edge of Ptuj from the North
- the river *Drau*, south of the Isle of Mur, which has 'waves of gold'; this is also true: in the Middle Ages gold was found in the Drau river
- *Styria*, today the southern part of Austria, extended a good deal further south at the time of Wolfram. It was also called Lammire after Gandin's daughter, Gahmuret's sister.

One further question on this subject occupied Viktor Stracke until his death. It concerned the 'Anschewein' or 'Anschau' dynasty, also called 'Anschouwe' by Wolfram, often falsely cited as 'Anjou'. The mix-up stems from the fact that the Anschau dynasty is seen in connection with an area surrounding the French town Angers, which is connected with the House of Anjou.

Many years ago already, anthroposophical researchers such as Ernst Uehli questioned this connection, specifically because high-ranking members of the Stauffer dynasty such as Friedrich Barbarossa, Friedrich II and Konradin, who were seen as supporters of the Grail stream, were in conflict with the representatives of the House of Anjou (Karl von Anjou had Konradin beheaded). A connection between the House of Anjou and the Parsifal dynasty is therefore completely out of the question.

Shortly before his death Viktor Stracke found a solution to this riddle. Today there is a castle near Rohasberg with the Slavonic name Poglet which, translated into German, means 'Anschau': 'Po' = 'An', 'glet' = 'schau'. This castle dates back to the 17th century, yet its foundations might go back to a much earlier time (as is true for example of the castle of Ptuj). Is it not possible that in the 9th century, or maybe even earlier, the dynasty of 'Anschau', the family on Parsifal's father's side, resided here?[48]

The Mystery Surrounding Rudolf Steiner's Birthplace

Of course this does not solve the question conclusively, but it may point to a possible solution.

Rudolf Steiner's date of birth

When this essay was first published the question of Rudolf Steiner's date of birth was the subject of debate. According to Rudolf Steiner's undated, brief handwritten autobiographical text, which he either did not complete, or the rest of which has not survived, it is clear that he was born on 25 February 1861 in Kraljevec: 'My birthday falls on 25 February 1861. I was baptized two days later.'

This facsimile text was first published at Easter 1975 in the *Beiträge zur Rudolf-Steiner-Gesamtausgabe* [supplement to the Complete Works] on the 50th anniversary of Rudolf Steiner's death. This booklet also reprints a further two letters by Eugenie von Bredow, from which it can be seen that she must, between February 1920 and February 1921, have discovered Rudolf Steiner's actual date of birth, since she congratulates him accordingly in her letter of 25 February 1921: 'Today, which in this incarnation of your individuality is said to be the day of your actual birth, whereas hitherto we always thought it to be 27 February...'

In the 19th century, particularly in isolated and rural Catholic communities, it was not unknown for the church or birth records to record the baptism rather than the actual birth. Why Rudolf Steiner did not correct this inaccuracy later and even kept up this long 'tradition', for example in Chapter One of his autobiography, initially remains a riddle, although various reasons might be cited.

First of all a mistake in the church records cannot be ruled out, and one can imagine that when Rudolf Steiner later noticed this inaccuracy he saw it as a clear sign from the spiritual world. In this way he was protected from possible abuse inflicted by unscrupulous occult circles. As he was the first initiate of modern times who worked completely in the open and publicly these dangers should not be underestimated.

It is also possible, seen from a higher perspective, that this intervention in his destiny was actually fully justified. As already mentioned, Rudolf Steiner was born on 25 February as a very weak child, and it was feared he might not survive. After two days this danger had passed and his survival was assured.

Spiritually this situation means that until his baptism on 27 February it was still uncertain whether Rudolf Steiner's entelechy would be able to remain in his body or whether it would have to withdraw again into the spiritual world. Not until two days after his birth did the spirit finally decide to incarnate and was now ready to take up the physical body as its future earthly instrument. Therefore Rudolf Steiner was quite right to speak later of 27 February as the day of his birth—although not in a physical sense.

The life of a high initiate, as Rudolf Steiner was, cannot be measured only by the normal criteria that are applied to an average human being. The earthly life of a true initiate is a Mystery which may only be wholly revealed to those of his own circle of leading initiates on earth.

4. A Path to Rudolf Steiner[49]

First encounter

On first meeting Rudolf Steiner's work one is surprised to find that his Complete Works contain over 350 books. It is astonishing to discover the competence with which he addresses many subjects and practical issues, particularly at a time when people had begun to develop greater specialism in every field. Since the Renaissance there have been very few universal scholars in European history. And now we find someone in the 20th century who moved confidently in all areas of knowledge. This is a fact we can discover simply from a first, superficial glance at his work.

When we also consider the *contents*, however, a further surprise emerges. His work consists almost exclusively of the results of spiritual research, carried out with a precision and thoroughness usually found only in the natural sciences. Yet the subject matter is not concerned with mundane matters but realities and beings of the spiritual world. And it all derives from Rudolf Steiner's own spiritual research. This begs the question how anyone could possibly have done this and, above all, how he himself did it.

Moving from this question to Rudolf Steiner's biography one soon notices that his life is in reality anthroposophy's greatest mystery. The path of development of its founder lies without doubt at its centre. Deeply astonished one sees the results of his spiritual work and now wishes to discover how he was able to achieve them.

In the ancient Mysteries the path into the spiritual world was never revealed to the uninitiated. Hardly ever and only in special circumstances was anything disclosed to the public. This situation, however, changed fundamentally with the raising of Lazarus when, for the first time in the history of the Mysteries, a full initiation process took place quite publicly instead of in the seclusion of a temple. Spiritually connecting to this event it was possible for Rudolf Steiner to tread the spiritual paths which correspond to today's level of human development, and also to lecture publicly about them.

In *Knowledge of the Higher Worlds* and other books, Rudolf Steiner describes in detail the path of modern initiation which allowed him to attain the results of his spiritual research. He himself pursued this path of initiation, only passing on to others what he had first thoroughly investigated and tested.

Today everything published by Rudolf Steiner in this domain is freely available because anthroposophy's highest ideal is individual freedom. Not without reason is anthroposophy founded on *The Philosophy of Freedom*.[50] Therefore, when taking the first steps on this path, a feeling of entire freedom ensues. One may carry on studying or, after a while, start with meditations or other spiritual exercises. During study we are already completely free. Rudolf Steiner emphasizes repeatedly that the spiritual facts communicated by him should be verified from all angles. The complicated forms of thought in which he expresses his research results were chosen specifically so that the reader can remain entirely free.

For anyone deciding to take up the anthroposophical schooling path a further step is possible, which will be discussed below.

The path

Seriously taking up the path of schooling involves a basic requirement, *trust*. If one does not possess this one should continue to study anthroposophy until one has gained a sufficient level of trust in the schooling path. When one notices how carefully Rudolf Steiner presents this path, how he makes one aware of the spiritual consequences of every step, then, as time goes by, the study of this path will impart sufficient trust in it to lead eventually to wanting to pursue it oneself. And when this happens it will become apparent that we are now on the same path that Rudolf Steiner *himself* explored for all of us. If he had not pursued it himself he would not have been able to pass it on. So we may say in all modesty that we are following in Rudolf Steiner's footsteps. However, we are only at the very beginning of this path on which he was able to go incomparably far. This means that objective trust in this path eventually becomes trust in Rudolf Steiner himself.

Thus the first fundamental requirement for a spiritual pupil is objective trust in this *path*. And the further one advances, the more one experiences Rudolf Steiner at one's side. Such a personal experience impresses itself on the soul. Through objective trust in the path an ever-deeper connection is found with the one who took it before us, and then made it available to everyone today. This is how inner trust in Rudolf Steiner can grow without turning him into a 'guru'. This objective trust in the spiritual teacher accords with complete personal freedom. One remains an autonomous modern human being yet is able to follow him on the spiritual path without surrendering the least bit of freedom.

As already mentioned, Rudolf Steiner speaks as follows about this kind of trust in the spiritual teacher, who on the modern Rosicrucian path gradually becomes the pupil's friend:

> With the Rosicrucian way the guru becomes more and more a friend whose authority is based on inner assent. The only possible relationship in this case is one of complete personal trust. The least distrust between teacher and pupil would break the bond that has to exist between them.[51]

Even in daily life true friendship is impossible without mutual trust. Rudolf Steiner also points out that every new spiritual capacity in humanity which can be nurtured and developed within the soul, has first to be attained by *one* human being. In this respect he mentions the individuality of Gautama Buddha who was, at the time, the first human being to pursue and describe to humanity the eightfold path; or also Aristotle who established logical thinking, still valid today, for all following generations.[52]

Something similar is valid for the modern Christian Rosicrucian path of initiation. Rudolf Steiner was the *first* to tread it through the spiritual forces of the present Michael epoch and then make it available for all people of good will. According to Rudolf Steiner not even the most advanced Rosicrucians were able to take this path in full consciousness.

> And this is the peculiarity since the beginning of the Michael epoch, since the end of the 1870s, the last third of the 19th century: what was attained in the way described above in the time of the old Rosicrucians, can now be attained in a conscious way.[53]

The truth

A second soul quality is necessary on the schooling path. This relates to the truthfulness of spiritual research. Before the Mystery of Golgotha the old Mysteries were mainly about spiritual wisdom, in which everything related to the content. This content is what the founders of religions and the old initiates tried to bring down to earth from the spiritual world. But with the arrival of the Christ an important change took place. From then onwards, instead of the 'what' of content, the prime focus shifts to the person of the seeker, the 'who'.

Fyodor M. Dostoevsky expressed this once in the following way: 'If I had to choose between the truth and the Christ then I would choose the Christ.' Maybe this initially sounds paradoxical. Did not Christ himself during his life on earth say: 'I am the truth'? Is there really a choice; is it not the same? No, it is not the same at all! Therefore it is of fundamental importance for mankind to choose the Christ. He is the *personification* of the truth, the truth that is at the same time *a being* and therefore ranks infinitely higher than any truth merely thought of.

With this question about the 'who' we uncover one of the deepest secrets of Christianity. In the post-Christian era the path to the truth is the path to Christ (and not *vice versa*) as humanity develops by integrating into itself something of this truth of the Christ.

As we have seen, Rudolf Steiner gave his whole life to researching the spiritual world, which is the world of truth. All of us, because we come from the spiritual world, carry something of it within us even if at first subconsciously. To become conscious of it is only possible, however, if the truth does not only imbue our consciousness but becomes integral to our being. The archetypal Christian principle is: 'I *am* the truth'. And the human being has to become this truth.

Whilst studying anthroposophy you meet the truth of the spiritual world in a form that is appropriate for today's consciousness soul. In other words, in Rudolf Steiner's supersensible research the truth of the spiritual world speaks directly to us. After a while the soul's embrace of this truth leads to a new relationship with Rudolf Steiner. He was only able to find this truth and pass it on because he embodied it.

How this new relationship with Rudolf Steiner can be shaped further can be understood from the following. On the path of schooling we first have to show, as is fitting for the modern consciousness soul, a healthy respect towards the objective truth we find in Rudolf Steiner's work, which gradually evolves into true and free devotion.

A child feels natural devotion for an older person, but is not free in this. And yet this childlike behaviour is of the utmost importance for later life. In his book *Knowledge of the Higher Worlds*, Rudolf Steiner describes how, out of childlike devotion, the force develops which later in life enables us to meet the truth in the only right way, that is, with devotion. This mood of devotion vis-à-vis the truth is *the* fundamental mood of the modern schooling path. In this book Rudolf Steiner describes many soul qualities necessary for humanity's spiritual development; yet the quality of devotion takes pride of place. He speaks about it for six pages, and again later in the book.

When we find that Rudolf Steiner, a modern Christian initiate, not only speaks about the spiritual world—at the same time the world of truth—in his many lectures and written works, but actually lived or embodied it as an individual, and thus became its representative on earth, our devotion to the truth gained through the schooling path can widen to encompass the truth acknowledged in the human being. This is no longer an old approach to devotion, leading to dependency on another person—even a high initiate. What is involved here is, rather, an objective devotion to the truth: a recognition that one can revere the other freely and independently of all external authority, because he himself is the bearer of this truth. In other words, we can revere Rudolf Steiner and yet remain autonomous and free. The one no longer negates the other.

In conclusion it can be said that we are concerned with lifelong development of the quality of devotion, as the foundation of any modern spiritual path of schooling.[54] Such a path consists of three stages: from unfree devotion during childhood to devotion to the truth at a more mature age; and finally a wholly new kind of devotion to those who have attained higher development and in whom the truth has become an inseparable part of their personality. Throughout his life Rudolf Steiner was deeply devoted to the great masters of esoteric Christianity without in the slightest compromising his freedom and absolute independence.

This also answers the question often posed as to whether Rudolf Steiner might have erred in his spiritual research. We are not concerned here with particulars but with a fundamental question. And the answer to it is this: He communicated responsibly and conscientiously, in a rigorously scientific way, *only as much* of the truth of the results of his spiritual research into the spiritual world as he himself could verify through the methods described in his books. Whenever he was not quite sure he remained silent and continued his research—sometimes for years—until he was ready to assume responsibility for his research before the spiritual world and thus before the truth in himself.

Out of this objective feeling of devotion to Rudolf Steiner, which leaves us completely free, arises a growing experience of his spiritual presence and willingness to help on the spiritual schooling path.

A new life

The third quality necessary on the schooling path is that of gratitude. This is also the sixth condition for a spiritual pupil.[55] In a healthy soul it arises by itself through a deep encounter with anthroposophy. If you look back over your own anthroposophical life you may ask what would have become of you *without* anthroposophy. What miserable existence would you have if you *had not* met it? Over the years this may give rise to the sure conviction that anthroposophy has given you a *new life*.

Our first encounter with anthroposophy is an especially important biographical moment. Looking back, everything that *preceded* this point seems like a kind of preparation for a new life. Rudolf Steiner points to this basic attribute of anthroposophy in the second letter to the members: 'Anthroposophy can only flourish as something living. The characteristic of her being is life. *She is life flowing from the spirit.* Therefore she has to be nurtured by the living soul, the warming heart.'[56] Rudolf Steiner speaks about a special moment where something like the following might happen. Someone is walking in the mountains without noticing that he is approaching a crevasse. Suddenly he hears someone calling 'Stop'. He looks around but nobody is there. And yet at this moment he has escaped certain death: if he had taken just one more step he would undoubtedly have fallen into the crevasse. Thus he has been given new life. Rudolf Steiner calls such an experience the 'call of Christian Rosenkreutz'.[57] Christian Rosenkreutz chooses his esoteric pupils through such a call.

But there are other occasions, which have similar consequences—occurring instead through one of Rudolf Steiner's books or lectures, maybe even in just one sentence. Here one also hears a call: not from without now, but from the innermost depths of the soul where the dead also speak to us. That is a call from Rudolf Steiner who gives us a new life when we meet anthroposophy. This call can of course be heard without first having to face a life-threatening situation.

This experience can awaken a completely new relationship to Rudolf Steiner within the soul, and arises out of the deepest *gratitude* to our destiny because we have been permitted to encounter anthroposophy in this life. Sooner or later everyone who does not have a merely superficial or intellectual grasp of anthroposophy, but encounters it in a deep, existential way, will sense the encounter as a blessing of destiny. Rudolf Steiner confirms this with the words: 'Whoever has the opportunity today to devote himself to spirit knowledge enjoys a gift of grace from karma.'[58] And the gratitude for this experience may extend to Rudolf Steiner himself. Because truly there would be no anthroposophy without him.

Thus our meeting with anthroposophy first leads to gratitude towards *our own destiny,* and later grows into a deep gratefulness to Rudolf Steiner. At the same time this gratefulness is without any obligation or the slightest danger of loss of independence. Gratefulness that has developed in this way is entirely objective because it is implicit in the very nature of its source. It is inextinguishably imprinted in our biography.

And when we have listened to Rudolf Steiner's spiritual call in full freedom and are willing to follow it, this means we are willing to accept the newly given life and address the tasks arising from it. Then Rudolf Steiner can speak to our inner being, and we are on the way to becoming his spiritual pupil.

The 'I Am'

As we have seen therefore, there are three qualities which we can instil in ourselves which primarily lead us to Rudolf Steiner today: *trust* in the anthroposophical schooling path, *devotion* to the truthfulness of anthroposophy and *gratitude* to the powers of destiny that have allowed us to meet anthroposophy.[59] But to successfully continue on this path an important further, fourth quality has to be added.

As we know, the mystery of the 'I' in the 'I am' is at the core of anthroposophy. When Rudolf Steiner was asked in London how anthroposophy might be briefly defined for the Oxford Dictionary he wrote in English: 'Anthroposophy is knowledge produced by the higher self in man.'[60] However, our higher self or higher ego is not within us. At birth it remains in the spiritual world and thus is found *outside* us.[61] What we usually call our ego or I is only a mirror image of our higher self within our bodily sheaths. If our real ego lies outside us how can we meet it during initiation? Anthroposophy answers this as follows: In everything that approaches us karmically from without, in blows of fate, in natural catastrophes which affect you personally, and particularly through what comes towards you from other people, the higher self works within you in an objective way.

This means that when someone looks for his higher self only *within himself* he falls subject to one of the greatest illusions, turns into a blatant egotist and in some cases may even fall into the clutches of black magic. However if he looks for it *outside himself* with full devotion and love, then gradually he learns to love *everything* that surrounds him, everything that he encounters in his earthly life.

The higher self is a purely spiritual being. And true love for it therefore is a selfless love for the spiritual manifest everywhere in the world, and in particular in other people. Without love of the higher self of the other we cannot find our own higher self in the spiritual world. Union with it, however, forms the core of modern initiation. Only at the level of intuition can a real encounter with the higher self take place in the spirit and lead to a unification of being. Intuition is, however, pure love which alone makes possible complete union with another, without losing oneself. Therefore, in order to really tread the path to the higher self, this selfless love is the primary quality required. 'What is revealed through intuition can be attained only by developing and spiritualizing to the highest degree the capacity for love. A person must be able to make this capacity for love into a cognitional force'[62]—that is, one which can be recognized by the higher self. Such a love that has become a higher force of knowledge is, again, in no way ego-less; it alone opens all the gates to the higher self and thus to our own true being.

The first encounter with the higher self in the spiritual world is not at all abstract but a real event. As long as we are unable to unite with our higher self out of our own forces of intuition, we depend on the help of those who have taken this path before us. Here Rudolf Steiner says something that many who only relate to spiritual science superficially may not like to hear. It is so important, though, that I wish to quote it here in full:

> The higher human self does not live within us, but around us ... We must seek it with those who have already trodden the path that we wish to tread ... If, in preparation for the future, we wish to approach it more closely, we must seek it above all in the company of those individualities who can work during the night on our etheric body.

And later in the same lecture Rudolf Steiner says even more specifically: 'The more highly developed individualities are the higher self.'[63] These words, however, can only be rightly understood by interpreting them from an esoteric point of view. It is especially important not to confuse the personal with the super-personal because the higher self quite objectively belongs to the latter sphere. Therefore spiritual love for Rudolf Steiner can only be of a selfless and super-personal character. This knowledge opens up a quite new perspective on our relationship with Rudolf Steiner, in which our love for him can be completely objective and free as we see in him the bearer of the higher self of all of his pupils who wish to pursue *his* path into the spiritual world. Thus is born a selfless love for the one who enables us to consciously recognize, *in him*, our higher self as future ideal. The higher self that we have to develop as the goal of all our endeavours is already fully real and present in him because he has taken the path which still lies ahead of us.

There is a danger, however, that those who have no experience whatsoever of their higher self succumb to the temptation to project what has been quoted above onto their own lower self and thus attempt to pull a high individuality like Rudolf Steiner down to their level. Then the encounter with the individuality of Rudolf Steiner is as hard to bear as that with their own higher self or the Guardian of the Threshold. However, the dissent voiced against Rudolf Steiner, which is born from this, only demonstrates that those concerned are not looking selflessly for their higher self in the spiritual world but only within themselves, and therefore they are unable to endure a real approach to him.

Here it is right to ask a further question: If Rudolf Steiner does indeed represent my higher self how can I remain a free human being? The answer lies in the mystery of the selfless, but not ego-less love that becomes the highest force of intuitive knowledge, and thus leads to the objective higher self on the path of modern spiritual pupilship. Here there is no question of any constraints on freedom. If it were otherwise, Rudolf Steiner would not have been able to stand before humanity as spiritual teacher in our present epoch.

In other words, without selfless and pure love for Rudolf Steiner we really cannot reach the goal of the path to our higher self as he gave it. We will only be completely free if our love for Rudolf Steiner has the quality required on the path of schooling.

At the same time this love for our higher self, which we can only find outside ourselves, will turn into a love towards everything in the world that is true, beautiful and good.[64] The closer we come to our higher self in the spiritual world, the stronger our love will be for the master whom we ourselves follow—in other words, whose footsteps we follow on this path into the higher worlds. Then we will meet him on this path coming not out of the past but from the future. And out of his strictly objective spiritual authority he will present us with the forces of our higher self long before we would otherwise be able to attain them ourselves—as an answer to our selfless love for him and without the least interference in our freedom.

It can be said categorically that the higher self of the human being—if properly approached—never interferes with individual freedom but instead elevates it to a totally new level—which Rudolf Steiner describes as 'new freedom'. In *Knowledge of the Higher Worlds* he ends the chapter on the encounter with the lesser Guardian of the Threshold—which we can only experience as spiritual pupil when we advance to a certain level of experience of our higher self—with the words: 'The experience of our new freedom outweighs all other feelings. And in the light of this experience, our new duties and responsibilities seem natural and inevitable as intrinsic to a given stage of life.' This new freedom was experienced by many in Rudolf Steiner's presence, in particular those who knew him personally, and many have told us about it verbally and in writing.

Considering the aforesaid we discover that the four steps describing our contemporary relationship with Rudolf Steiner embody a deeply Christian process. They are the microcosmic image of Christ's words: 'I am the way, the truth and the life' (John. 14, 6). An inner approach to the spiritual reality of these words can be developed through anthroposophy by

1. Trust in the schooling *path*
2. Devotion to its *truthfulness*
3. Gratitude for its transformative effect on our whole *life* and for what culminates from these three qualities
4. Selfless *love* for our higher *self*.

If we take up *this* path to our higher self we will also find that it gives rise to a new and intimate relationship with Rudolf Steiner, which does not impinge on our individual freedom. Then we can recognize that the words: 'I am the way, the truth and the life' form an indispensable foundation not only for the modern schooling path but also for the right relationship with our teacher who, as the leading Christian initiate of our time, precedes us in following Christ.

But the decision to tread this path has to arise out of our own initiative. Nobody else can awaken in us the trust, devotion, gratefulness and love for our higher self. And when, on this path and *in this way,* we seek to nurture our relationship with Rudolf Steiner, we will soon find that he *accompanies* us through our trust in him, *helps* us because of our devotion, *speaks* to us because of our gratitude, and *grants* us the forces of our higher self which approach us from the future because of our selfless love for him.

Our experience will increasingly show us what it means to be Rudolf Steiner's esoteric pupil. Then Benedictus's words from the Mystery Drama, which describe Rudolf Steiner's relationship to all his true pupils, become a reality and certain truth:

> I must accompany each one
> who has received from me on earth
> the spirit's light, whether he knew or not
> that he became my pupil.
> I have to lead him further on the way
> which he through me began to walk in spirit.[65]

These words written for Benedictus in 1912 can be understood in a deeper sense since the Christmas Foundation Meeting. It was then that Rudolf Steiner freely and ego-consciously—that is to say integrated with his own karma—united himself with the Anthroposophical Society. With this sacrifice he wanted to give his pupils the opportunity to follow his Christ-imbued *I*, which on earth established the anthroposophical schooling *path*, gave humanity the *truthfulness* of anthroposophy, and whose *life forces* made possible the development of manifold practical initiatives. Thus, through Society members' free ego forces, every aspect of the path, the truth and the life of anthroposophy could thrive and prosper.

At the Christmas Foundation Meeting, therefore, Rudolf Steiner gave Society members the supersensible Foundation Stone as a solid foundation for the Anthroposophical Society. This contains the mystery of the new spiritual epiphany of which he spoke many years previously in his book *Theosophy*: 'The spirit forming an "I" and living as the "I" will be called *spirit self* because it manifests as the "I", or ego, or self of man.' For those who have planted it in their hearts, this *epiphanic* spirit appears in the thought aura of the dodecahedral stone of love,[66] transforms its light of thought into the spiritual *path*, its imaginative form into the new *truth* and its substance of love into the source of spiritual *life* that can sustain and permeate the Anthroposophical Society.[67]

And thus may this spiritual Foundation Stone of the Anthroposophical Society, which holds the mystery of the Christ words 'I am the way, the truth and the life'—because it was formed from these I-words—be an eternal link to Rudolf Steiner so that his aims become ours as he himself made Christ's will his own.

5. Rudolf Steiner and the Founding Executive Council[68]

The esoteric triangle

Looking at the constellation of those invested by Rudolf Steiner at the Christmas Foundation Meeting as members of the esoteric council, one notices that the latter consists of an inner and an outer circle. To the inner circle belong: Marie Steiner, Ita Wegman and Albert Steffen, while Elisabeth Vreede and Guenther Wachsmuth belong to the outer circle. Rudolf Steiner is at the centre of both circles. He is the spiritual teacher and head of the esoteric School and the leader of the Anthroposophical Society.

In a private conversation Rudolf Steiner describes the 'spiritual triangle within the pentagram'[69] as an esoteric figure forming the inner constellation of the founding council.

As already outlined in detail in an earlier work by the author,[70] Rudolf Steiner's words can be understood as follows:

The spiritual triangle of the esoteric constellation of the founding council:

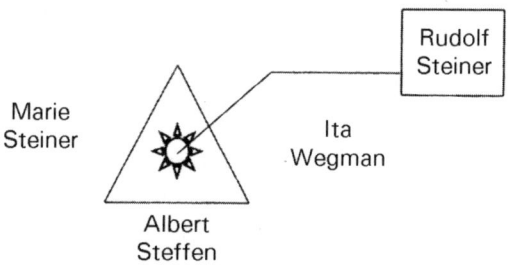

Its exoteric constellation, which points towards activity in the outer world, forms a pentagram:

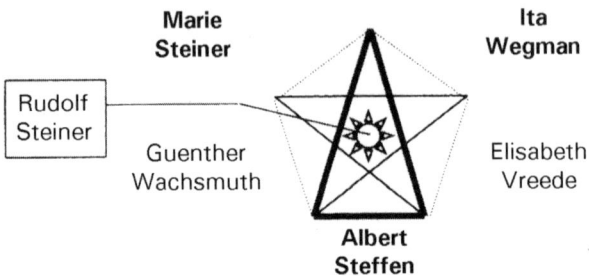

The names in the drawing do not relate to the corners but to the sides of the figures.

What is the meaning of the esoteric triangle around Rudolf Steiner in the founding council? Its task is to form a spiritual sheath composed of the forces of the three individualities who constitute its form, so as to protect the teacher on earth and enable him to be supersensibly present after his death. Thus he could work through the above-named council members to participate in spiritual leadership of the esoteric School and the Anthroposophical Society.

We can only understand the nature of this esoteric sheath by means of its highest macrocosmic archetype, of which Rudolf Steiner spoke in his lectures of 30 May 1912. According to him, the three sheaths of the Christ Ego, as highest group-ego of mankind, have gradually to be formed through the moral deeds of mankind during its further evolution on earth. His spiritual-physical sheath has to evolve out of human conscience; His etheric sheath out of deeds of love and compassion, and the astral sheath 'out of all moral deeds of wonder, trust, reverence and belief, in short through everything that belongs to the supersensible path of knowledge'. This human collaboration with Christ will last until the end of earth evolution. Initially the Christ impulse, which united with earth evolution at the Mystery of Golgotha, 'had nothing to clothe itself with on earth'. According to Rudolf Steiner, He will only acquire His new sheaths through humanity's further evolution on earth, so that by the end of their evolution these sheaths become the spiritual centre for all humanity (its true I) around which they will unite in their full diversity. 'Thus throughout earth's evolution, the human being will create a great community that can be filled through and through with the Christ impulse.'

What has to become reality in the future for all humanity can already be prepared today within a smaller group of those who, through their true Christian initiation, possess full Christ consciousness on earth, i.e. who in their individual I have absorbed something of the universal I of the Christ.[71]

This was precisely what had to occur in Rudolf Steiner's ego on a microcosmic, human level during his lifetime; and was to continue after his death thanks to the shared esoteric work of Marie Steiner, Ita Wegman and Albert Steffen within the founding council.

Marie Steiner

From the very beginning of their collaboration, Marie Steiner's main esoteric task was to create a 'spiritual-*physical*' sheath around Rudolf Steiner for all his ensuing spiritual work on earth. Rudolf Steiner's main stipulation, when asked to lead the newly founded German Section of the Theosophical Society (1902), was therefore that Marie von Sivers would be involved in this leadership. He handed her the section's administrative work, which allowed him to concentrate all his energies on his spiritual-scientific and esoteric task. Rudolf Steiner himself remembers this as follows:

> During these lectures [on medieval mysticism, which he gave during the winter of 1900 at the Earl of Brockdorff's theosophical meetings] there appeared one day in the audience Marie von Sivers, who was chosen by destiny at that time to take into her capable hands the German section of the Theosophical Society, founded soon after the beginning of my lecturing activity.[72]

And in the Theosophical Society's most influential German magazine *Vâhan*, Rudolf Steiner published the following notice: 'From 20 September [1902], Miss M. von Sivers is taking on all administrative matters of the German Theosophical Society and the library.'[73] This enabled Rudolf Steiner to remain true to the most important 'occult law' according to which an initiate is not permitted to mix his spiritual work with administrative or organizational matters.[74]

In addition, Marie Steiner took on the sacrificial and protective role of preventing too much pressure impinging on and impairing Rudolf Steiner's esoteric work in the form of wishes and demands from members of the Anthroposophical Society and others. For this reason he sometimes called her his 'spiritual cleaner' and emphasized repeatedly how grateful he was for her help, i.e. for the protective spiritual-physical sheath she had provided.

In a deeper sense, in his immediate surroundings, Marie Steiner became a kind of 'cosmic conscience' whose actions resembled a 'cosmic court of justice'—often with catastrophic results for those who sought access to Rudolf Steiner with impure or selfish agendas. She was the only one near him who had the strength to say 'no' to someone who approached Rudolf Steiner inappropriately. She always tried to shield him, like a spiritual wall, from all negative influences and hindrances that could distract him from his spiritual work. Even when her uncompromising protection of Rudolf Steiner earned her hostility, she freely accepted this task to the end.

This throws a special light on the first meeting between Marie von Sivers and Rudolf Steiner. From the first moment, as if following the inner voice of a higher conscience, she recognized in him the carrier of the main task of esoteric Christianity for our time and decided to devote all her talents and forces to his mission. She held on to this inner certainty to the end of her life. This is why Rudolf Steiner wrote to her shortly before his death: 'Because I accord inner competence as regards myself only to *your* judgement'.[75]

Maybe the characteristic capacity here is her complete altruism. The Russian eurythmist Tatjana Kisseleff, who worked under Marie Steiner for many years, recalls:

> I experienced altruism as a fundamental aspect of her being: a bearer of the highest, super-personal, spiritual aims. Where others sometimes felt arbitrariness, subjectivity, injustice, lack of knowledge or human insight, I found that it was as if, through Marie Steiner's intercession, a cosmic decision was made, a cosmic council was held.'[76]

In Rudolf Steiner's eyes she was a spiritual 'priestess'[77] who, bound by her destiny, guarded the invisible altar of the higher worlds where he served the spirit. Her honest character, incorruptible sense of truth and especially her immense soul forces formed a firm basis for this difficult task. In a conversation with Klara Walter, Rudolf Steiner once said about the spiritual forces gathered behind her: 'Yes, you must understand ... a strong force stands behind her, that is what many cannot endure.'[78]

Marie Steiner needed this exceptional spiritual force to create a spiritual-physical sheath for the teacher, drawing on the forces of a conscience strong enough to protect him from occult blows and attacks. Like no other in his surroundings she knew of the relentless hostility against him from some secret occult Masonic lodges and members of the Jesuits, and the real, even life-threatening dangers emanating from them.[79]

Ita Wegman

Ita Wegman represented a completely different impulse in the circles around Rudolf Steiner. Within the esoteric council it was her task to form the etheric sheath around him, out of the purest forces of compassion and love, which contained the healing forces necessary for his spiritual work. Her professional capacity as a doctor was of special use when fulfilling this difficult task. During the last years of his earthly life Rudolf Steiner relied particularly on the forces of her compassionate love for his spiritual work. In his letter to Ita Wegman dated 14 June 1924 he wrote: 'I meditate in your meditation and I rely on your love.'[80]

Ita Wegman, who had been part of the anthroposophical movement since its earliest beginnings—she became a member of the German Section of the Theosophical Society and had already met Rudolf Steiner in Berlin in 1902—did not experience her spiritual awakening until the burning of the first Goetheanum. When she saw the mighty flames blazing in the darkened sky, her inner life not only opened up to the connection between the first Goetheanum and the Artemis Temple in Ephesus, but she also became aware of her own karmic relationship with Rudolf Steiner, which went back to their joint incarnation during the Ephesus Mysteries and before. From this moment onwards, guided by feelings of love and compassion for the teacher, she decided to dedicate her work and life completely to Rudolf Steiner and told him so during a lecture cycle in Penmaenmawr in 1923.

Thus the meeting took place on earth between the teacher and his most important pupil, who had accompanied him during many earthly incarnations and whose awakening led to the shared spiritual work that was to become the start of the renewal of the whole anthroposophical impulse, and was completed with the Christmas Foundation Meeting.

This free decision by Rudolf Steiner's most important pupil who, following this great tragedy, offered him all her forces and capacities for sacrificial love and boundless compassion through the recognition of karma, allowed Rudolf Steiner to research completely new areas of the spiritual world and to lead the anthroposophical movement in an entirely different way.

It also enabled Rudolf Steiner to use the forces of his own love for this pupil when he saw how, in the spiritual world, the anthroposophical movement's leading Michaelic powers looked down with increasingly good will upon the renewed alliance, rooted as it was in their long karmic connection. Thus Rudolf Steiner wrote in his letter to Ita Wegman dated 11 June 1924:

> Now it is also granted to me to speak differently to people than I did before. The spiritual powers, who come to expression in anthroposophy, look kindly, lovingly on how I lean on the love of your so greatly appreciated soul. This is my greatest support.[81]

Out of this sacrificial love and compassion, which grew even deeper after the teacher became ill, Ita Wegman was able to create a protective and healing sheath around Rudolf Steiner, which was strong enough to protect him from those demons to whose attacks he was particularly exposed during his illness and whose presence she experienced so strongly. Ita Wegman wrote: 'Demons that appeared threateningly. Many of these threats I knew, partly I understood, partly I did not. To understand it all would have been terrible, and so it remained secret.'[82]

And yet it would have been part of Ita Wegman's task to bravely counter this terrible reality face-to-face, thus standing at her teacher's side in this invisible fight.[83]

Albert Steffen

Albert Steffen, a great poet and exceptionally sensitive spiritual scientist, belonged to the few pupils around Rudolf Steiner who had his own personal spiritual experiences. Therefore Rudolf Steiner said of him that not only anthroposophists but also anthroposophy itself could learn a great deal from Albert Steffen about real paths into the spiritual world.

Less than forty days before his death Rudolf Steiner wrote about him:

> He [Steffen] does not have to learn from anthroposophy how to enter the spiritual world. But anthroposophy can experience through him a living 'pilgrim's journey' predisposed in the soul. Such a poetic spirit, if he is to be correctly understood, has to be met within the anthroposophical movement as the bearer of a message from the sphere of the spirit. We have to regard it as beneficent destiny that he wishes to be active within this movement.[84]

In Albert Steffen there lived, according to Rudolf Steiner in the same essay, 'the light of this truth', the truth of anthroposophy itself.

Such a light of anthroposophical truth works in the pure astral light of someone who has a natural disposition and, later, a consciously self-instilled sense of wonder, reverence and belief in the spiritual world and spiritual science, creatively and reverently experiencing its content within his soul. This soul quality can be felt not only in Albert Steffen's artistic work—his writings, drama and poetry—but also in his paintings, particularly his watercolours. They are comparable to the way an incredibly wise child might see the world, full of wonder for the mysteries of existence and most finely sensitive to the ubiquitous deeds of the supersensible world and the spiritual beings within it. Above all the gift for composition, unique to Albert Steffen, with its truly imaginative character—his water colours cannot be mistaken for those of another artist—his special feeling for colour and the ability to express through painting his ever-present, unshakeable trust in the good forces of existence, and the deeply held Manichean belief in their eventual victory, such as only a child or a great and wise man has, all demonstrate these great qualities of soul which Albert Steffen possessed.

Albert Steffen did not only harbour these feelings for spiritual science but also—and in particular—for his teacher. Out of these feelings was that shining imagination born in his soul, of which he spoke in his memorial address at Rudolf Steiner's funeral:

> ...Then this picture rose before me: the universe flooded with light, an endless ocean of sunlight which cast up forever soft and gentle undulations, waves that might well have been the wings of angels.
>
> This glowing life of the sun I beheld before my eyes, and I saw before it the chalice of the crescent moon, as a smiling face, a face eternally young—the countenance of Rudolf Steiner. It looked into the sun; it exchanged words with the sun.
>
> His head, which had been to its last moment a sacred vessel of thoughts, and his heart, which all his life through was filled with love at every beat, appeared to me as the immaculate moon and the loving sun.
>
> That which Rudolf Steiner wished to the last to keep within his body, in order to serve us—he the servant of God—that fully conscious thinking and that heart glowing with love—these twain stood in the spiritual sky as brother and sister.
>
> And when I saw this, I said to myself, 'Never again shall we fall into the habits of this dark century. However fearfully untruth, unloveliness, and evil may assail us, these forces shall never again lay hold upon us in our innermost being so long as we lift our spirits to this picture, and bathe ourselves in it and make it our elixir of life.
>
> For this is the Grail and Rudolf Steiner the fulfilment of Parsifal.[85]

If one really enters into this truly experienced imagination of Albert Steffen then one can feel how those spiritual forces of his soul that granted him this perception were precisely those forces that assigned him responsibility within the esoteric council for the third sheath, the astral sheath of Rudolf Steiner's ego.

The special constellation of soul qualities

Viewed in terms of their mutually complementary soul-spiritual qualities, the unique opportunity arising out of the joint work of the three main founding members on the council becomes apparent when one observes the way these three forces work together within the human soul.

From this perspective Marie Steiner represents the working of the forces of *thinking within the will* which, according to Rudolf Steiner's spiritual indications, is the *magic* constellation of the human soul. Thus the individuality of Marie Steiner worked magically on the people around her, and they experienced this as something superhuman. The forces of her feeling realm formed something like an inner space so as to call forth and develop thinking–will impulses in her soul. It can be said that the forces of feeling worked into her from the periphery, whilst thinking and will emanated from the core of her inner being, i.e. from her ego.

With Ita Wegman in contrast, the thinking forces worked mainly from the periphery whilst from the centre of her ego the *will and feeling* forces were active. This represented in her soul an *initiation* constellation, which she brought with her from earlier incarnations. This is why Rudolf Steiner made her joint leader of the First Class of the esoteric School.[86]

Finally, in the soul of Albert Steffen, worked will forces from the periphery and *feeling and thinking forces* through his ego, giving him a special disposition for the development of the new *conscious clairvoyance*, which during his life as poet was ever present in his creative imagination.

These three personalities in their totality represent the three main aspects of all true Mysteries of which Rudolf Steiner said the following:

> In all former occult schools there were three ways of ascending to the highest regions of perception. The first was that of initiation; the second of clairvoyance; the third of magic. These are three totally different things—initiation, clairvoyance, magic.[87]

What has been said above will now be illustrated by examples drawn from the lives of Marie Steiner, Ita Wegman and Albert Steffen. Many people's reminiscences refer to Marie Steiner truly possessing a certain magical force, which worked on the people around her so that after an encounter with her many had the impression that a certain higher, superhuman being was working through her.[88] This led to people around her either becoming friends or admirers; or the opposite: enemies. Hardly anyone could avoid these inner forces coming towards them.

From this came her special relationship to the Christ impulse which, at the very beginning of Rudolf Steiner's anthroposophical activity, enabled her to put the decisive question to him about the necessity of penetrating theosophical wisdom with Christian esotericism, i.e. how theosophy could 'take account of the Christ impulse'. Marie Steiner's special soul quality also resulted in her deep connection to Novalis and his magical idealism, which was neither founded on a logical-theological nor a mystical comprehension of the Christ but on a very special 'magical' access to Him, which mankind will achieve in the future.

The following incident shows that Marie Steiner had possessed these magical forces from her youth. During a lonely walk in the forest, Marie and her friends once ran into a pack of hungry wild dogs, which ran at them with loud barking and snarling. In order to protect her friends, Marie stepped in front of them and blocked the path. At this moment of greatest danger she experienced within herself a feeling of complete calm, out of which grew an inner force that put the dogs to flight.[89]

One of the many events in Ita Wegman's life, which certainly has the character of a true initiation, i.e. the awakening of someone on the threshold to the spiritual world, or, equally, on the threshold of death, happened during her serious illness in the year 1934. At the moment when she stood on the threshold to the spiritual world she experienced, according to her own words, a meeting with the Christ Being and with Rudolf Steiner, 'who sent me back to earth and expected of me that I do something different.'[90] In other words they expected of Ita Wegman that from this moment onwards she would begin to act out of her understanding of the essence of her initiation and her impulses on earth. Although this initiation experience happened after Rudolf Steiner's death, the foundation for it was laid during his lifetime because of the inner foundation of their relationship.

There are numerous examples of Albert Steffen's spiritual experiences, and it is sufficient to mention one that happened during the 'Sacraments of the Act of Consecration of Man' at the founding of the Christian Community on 16 September 1922 in the white room of the first Goetheanum. In his diary Albert Steffen describes this event as follows:

> Today the first Act of the Consecration of Man took place as a deed performed out of the spirit, where the resurrected Christ was present ... I may say that Christ was present because I saw his resurrection body of light and life when the words about the bread and the wine were spoken. This is the first time that I saw Christ as a Being before me.[91]

Thus these three individualities around Rudolf Steiner were to represent the three main directions of all true Mysteries as the basis for a renewed impulse given by Rudolf Steiner.

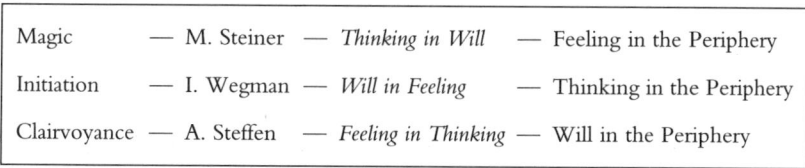

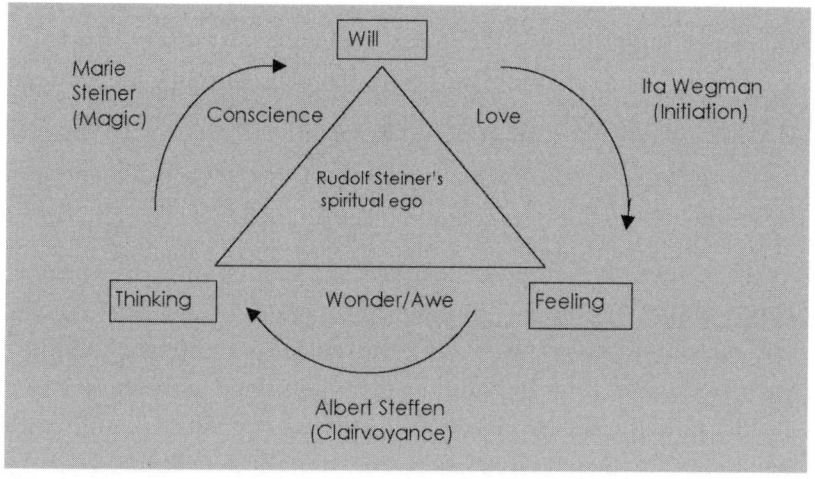

Only with this extraordinary constellation of soul qualities and with the harmonious collaboration and interaction between these three brilliant and at the same time polar opposite individuals, could a unique soul-spiritual vessel have been created for the reception of inspirations flowing from Rudolf Steiner's spiritual ego, even after his physical death.

For this, the work of this inner circle was extended by that of the other two personalities, Elisabeth Vreede and Guenther Wachsmuth (and possibly a further person, who has not been named)[92] in order also to ensure the exoteric leadership of the Anthroposophical Society.

The path to Rudolf Steiner today

From the above we can see that the founding council was selected as an archetype of a new, esoteric community that would work with Rudolf Steiner, regardless of whether he is incarnated on earth in a new incarnation or remains in the spiritual world. Although this council tragically was not able to fulfil this task, Rudolf Steiner's underlying archetype remains in force to this day, provided anthroposophists, of their own free will, are prepared to make it a reality on earth.[93]

In other words, even today Rudolf Steiner's pupils can create the described three sheaths as vessel on earth for their teacher's deeds from the spiritual world. According to Rudolf Steiner, this highest archetype of occult-social activity, given by the Christ to all humanity, will hold good until the end of earth evolution. In other words, its microcosmic, human form can become reality through the spiritual understanding and sacrificial will of those striving towards him.

When we create these soul-spiritual sheaths for Rudolf Steiner's ego we embark on a path that leads to us experiencing his individuality in our time. That is a true path towards the spiritual individuality of Rudolf Steiner. And at the same time it is a modern path to Christ, as Christ's words, 'Verily I say unto you, inasmuch as ye have done it unto one of the least of these my brethren, ye have done it unto me' (Mathew 25, 40), finds its full meaning when one speaks about a true Christian initiate, the bearer of an imprint of the Christ I and thus a true human representative of the Christ impulse on earth.[94]

Today anthroposophists are able to learn to consciously work at a microcosmic level on what, by the end of earth evolution, will be the reality for all of humanity, when everyone will be imbued with the Christ impulse.

PART II

The Mystery of the Laying of the Foundation Stone

1. Laying the Foundation Stone in 1923 as a Mystery Event[95]

The essence of Christianity

In his description of the esoteric foundations of Christianity, Rudolf Steiner repeatedly emphasizes that its essence does not lie in the revelation of new wisdom but in a unique creative act, which changed the connections between the earthly and the spiritual world. This is the Mystery of Golgotha: 'His Resurrection is the coming to birth of a new member or dimension of human nature—an incorruptible body.'[96]

At the turning point of time, Paul the apostle expressed this basic truth about Christianity with his incisive statement: 'And if Christ be not risen, then is our preaching vain, and your faith is also vain' (1. Cor. 15, 14). At the same time, this points to what distinguishes Christianity from all other world religions, which are all religions of wisdom: Christianity, from the very outset, is a universal historical reality since it is founded on a unique deed that has momentous significance for the whole world. This deed is also the source of all new, creative forces in the universe. Therefore Rudolf Steiner is able to say that Christianity begins as a religion but is in its essence greater than all religions. It supersedes the religious principle as such by far because 'Christianity is far greater than the religious principle itself.'[97]

It follows that every true Christian initiate, if he wishes to connect to the Mystery of Golgotha's source of strength, does not just convey new insights about its essence but more importantly has to become creative out of it. And because the Mystery of Golgotha, as the highest creative deed, took place at the same time in two worlds, the physical and the supersensible, such an initiate also becomes active out of the sources of both worlds.

Laying the Foundation Stone: a deed born of freedom and love

The above shows why, from its beginnings, anthroposophy was not just a theory but increasingly brought forth practical fruits in different fields of life, in particular in science, art, the social sphere and religion. These practical fruits of anthroposophy are today openly available to the world. They have led, and still do, to numerous new initiatives within contemporary culture.

More mysterious, however, because they are not immediately recognizable, are a Christian initiate's creative deeds drawn from the source of the Mystery of Golgotha in the spiritual world. Today we can only guess at how extensive Rudolf Steiner's purely spiritual deed was in reality. If his visible, earthly deeds, particularly towards the end of his life, took on a scale that was already close to superhuman, the question remains as to how far-reaching and important his spiritual deed was, which he carried out beyond the threshold of the spiritual world—not only for humanity but also for the world of the hierarchies.

We can recognize one such spiritual deed with our normal consciousness, and perhaps even freely participate in it. This creative deed forms the esoteric focus of the Christmas Foundation Meeting of 1923/1924 and is noted in the programme of the morning of 25 December 1923 as 'The laying of the Foundation Stone of the General Anthroposophical Society by Dr Rudolf Steiner.'

The address given on this occasion has been passed down to us as a shorthand note. On first reading one could be forgiven for thinking that this was an esoteric lesson, which Rudolf Steiner gave to members of the newly founded Anthroposophical Society. Looking more closely at this short text one soon realizes that it contains much more. An esoteric lesson primarily consists of the imparting of spiritual truths, which the initiate passes on in a form that leads in a particular way to inner transformation in the listening audience.

During the laying of the Foundation Stone, Rudolf Steiner primarily imparts such wisdom by pointing to one of his greatest spiritual-scientific research findings, which really opened up a new epoch of spiritual knowledge to humanity. This is his discovery of the archetype of the human being constituted of spirit, soul and body, which reveals how soul-spiritual forces and processes manifest in the earthly world within the three systems of our physical body.

Based on this knowledge, Rudolf Steiner now takes a decisive further step. And thus, from a certain moment in his address, he begins to describe in simple words what he himself at the same time performs as a spiritual *deed* in the spiritual world bordering the earth. This is the creation of a supersensible Foundation Stone, which he also calls the 'Dodecahedral Foundation Stone of Love'. Its creation is the freest and most individual act of creation through Rudolf Steiner's ego forces, an act whose essence points to his relationship—as the leading initiate of our time—to the Mystery of Golgotha. More than all else, this free creative deed most clearly shows Rudolf Steiner's deep relationship to the Mystery of Golgotha.

Just as Christ, as the only God to appear in human form on earth, accomplished his sacrifice at Golgotha in complete freedom and the highest love, so every human being who wishes to follow Him must, sooner or later, become active on earth out of these two forces. The earth's goal consists in the creation of a new humanity as the tenth hierarchy, which will become active in the cosmos out of freedom and love. And to lay the foundation for this future, and at the same time to offer an example, Christ performed his central deed on earth out of these two forces as 'a God who out of his own free will, out of love, accomplished the act whereby the earth and humanity could reach their goal.'[98]

Following this example, every Christian initiate who has developed his ego to full freedom and maturity can perform a similar deed. In other words, what Christ accomplished macrocosmically at the turning point of time, can be achieved microcosmically by every human being since the beginning of the epoch of the consciousness soul. The creation of the Foundation Stone at the Christmas Foundation Meeting can be seen as such a step. Only when viewed as such can Rudolf Steiner's creative deed be understood as the first human deed out of the forces of the tenth hierarchy. Therefore the fruit of this *free deed* is the Foundation Stone of *love*.

A further deed followed from this direct connection with the Mystery of Golgotha: the creation of the Foundation Stone. At the very moment when its conception was complete, Rudolf Steiner handed this, his greatest creation, to the members of the newly founded Anthroposophical Society. With the help of spiritual science we can imagine this process as follows: the spiritual Foundation Stone, during the process of its conception, already bore within it the possibility of multiplication according to the laws of spiritual economy, so that all members were given the opportunity to plant its spiritual image in the depths of their hearts.

With this 'multiplication' of its substance, Rudolf Steiner connected directly to the event at the turning point of time preceding the Mystery of Golgotha: the sharing of bread and wine with Christ's disciples at the Last Supper. Rudolf Steiner's deed was enacted in a different form however—because it occurred after the Mystery of Golgotha—so that it fully corresponds to today's level of human development. A new, purely spiritual Last Supper was founded at which all can participate in complete freedom. How participation at this purely spiritual Last Supper can lead to a true spiritual communion I have already described elsewhere.[99]

Foundation of a new human community

In the process described here it is of critical importance to note that, after being spiritually implanted in human hearts, the Foundation Stone can only continue to exist and prosper if it is understood and realized as the foundation for a new human community. Rudolf Steiner points to this reality at the laying of the Foundation Stone with the following words:

> Let us at this moment give form in our souls to the dodecahedral Foundation Stone which we lower into the soil of our souls so that it may remain there as a powerful sign in the strong foundations of our soul existence and so that in the future work of the Anthroposophical Society we may stand on this firm Foundation Stone.[100]

For the first time in the epoch of the consciousness soul, a fundamentally new community was founded on earth whose essence lies in the social realization of the words: 'My kingdom is not of this world.' (John. 18, 36). Rudolf Steiner comments on these words of Christ as follows: 'The kingdom of Christ Jesus is not of this world, but it must work in this world and human souls must be instruments of the kingdom that is not of this world.'[101] Realizing this goal will give rise

Laying the Foundation Stone in 1923 as a Mystery Event 63

to a human community on earth which, on the one hand, is completely open, i.e. fully integrated into present earth civilization with all its needs and questions, but at the same time has its spiritual roots and its esoteric basis in something that is not of this world but derives directly from the kingdom of Christ, which He wants to build in the midst of this world. And this foundation in our case is the supersensible Foundation Stone.

Rudolf Steiner constituted the General Anthroposophical Society, giving it a completely new and unique task: 'We must be absolutely clear that our Society, above all others, will have the task of combining the greatest conceivable openness with true and genuine esotericism.'[102]

In line with this task, the public character of the Anthroposophical Society is part of its complete integration into modern civilization (including its official registration with the companies register); and the esotericism cultivated within it involves, not least, that members stand together on the supersensible Foundation Stone created from the forces of Christ's kingdom.

'And the light shines in the darkness'

Within the human heart the Foundation Stone becomes the source of new inner strength revealed in two qualities: in spiritual light and spiritual warmth. These were permeated by Rudolf Steiner at the laying of the Foundation Stone with macrocosmic light and macrocosmic warmth, which at the turning point of time entered into humanity through the Christ, thus giving human beings the strength from then onwards to carry these forces into the world—and thus also into the darkness of today's civilization as a new light. At the laying of the Foundation Stone itself, Rudolf Steiner describes this process in the following words:

> And we can best strengthen this warmth of soul and this light of soul we need when we enliven them with that warmth and light that shone at the turning point of time as the Christ light in the world darkness.

And thus:

> This archetypal Holy Night that took place two thousand years ago ... may help us when we carry into the world what shines towards us through the thought-light of ... the dodecahedral Foundation Stone of love.

In this way Rudolf Steiner connects to the third theme of the turning point of time which is described in the prologue of the Gospel of St John: 'And the light shineth in darkness; and the darkness comprehended it not' (1,5). And to this day the Anthroposophical Society stands in the midst of our civilization, which on the eve of Ahriman's incarnation is increasingly filled with darkness and thus is less and less capable of understanding, let alone absorbing, the light of anthroposophy.

And yet one of the Anthroposophical Society's most central tasks involves bravely carrying this 'thought-light' of spiritual knowledge, despite all resistance and difficulties, into the darkness of today's civilization. This, however, will only be successful when members of the Anthroposophical Society do not forget its esoteric roots but stand unshakeably firm on its spiritual Foundation Stone—which belongs to the kingdom of Christ—and base all their work in the world upon it.

The secret of the Christmas Foundation Meeting

In conclusion it can be said that with these three steps Rudolf Steiner connects to the three events at the turning point of time. But because this connection actually takes place in the spiritual world where time runs in the opposite direction, Rudolf Steiner applies them in a reverse order in his own deeds. First he connects to the Mystery of Golgotha, then out of the source of its strength he connects to the Last Supper and finally to the appearance of the Christ light in the darkness of our earth, which today manifests in His reappearance in the etheric realm

This threefold path—from the *Word,* which as universal Word permeates the Mystery of Golgotha, to the *Life,* which is given to humanity at the Last Supper, to the *Light,* shining into today's darkness—corresponds to the three stages of the laying of the Foundation Stone at the Christmas Foundation Meeting: the creation of the Foundation Stone, the handing of its images to the members of the

Anthroposophical Society and the task arising from this of carrying its thought-light into the darkness of contemporary civilization.

What I have presented here is a further attempt to approach the mystery of the Christmas Foundation Meeting, which lies in what Rudolf Steiner described with the words 'cosmic turning point of time'. Just as he directly connected the Christmas Foundation Meeting to the archetypal Holy Night and thus, in an esoteric sense, to the Mystery of Golgotha, so today we can, in complete freedom, connect to his deed of love so as to continue working within the stream of the new Mysteries. These derive from the turning point of time, and entered modern consciousness at the Christmas Foundation Meeting.

2. The New Community

Humanity's temple

The spiritual process of connecting to the events at the turning point of time, which took place at the laying of the Foundation Stone on 25 December 1923, had further consequences for the life of the Anthroposophical Society. On the last day of the Christmas Foundation Meeting, Rudolf Steiner characterized these consequences as follows: 'We have here laid the Foundation Stone. On this Foundation Stone shall be erected the building whose individual stones will be the work achieved in all our groups by the individuals outside in the wide world.'[103] Here it has to be understood, however, that with the term 'groups' of the General Anthroposophical Society, Rudolf Steiner meant all communities working in its name, from study groups to national Societies. Out of this wide-ranging spiritual work occurring in the world through the Anthroposophical Society, a spiritual 'building' gradually has to arise that finds its roots and foundation within the supersensible Foundation Stone of love.

Thus Rudolf Steiner connected anew to something he had already endeavoured to realize in the years when he was developing the anthroposophical movement, and which true Rosicrucian esotericism regarded as a noble ideal. Rudolf Steiner points to this secret during the inauguration of the Christian Rosenkreutz branch in Neufchâtel. Both lectures held there close with the words: 'May this group be one of the building stones in the temple we wish to raise.'[104] What Rudolf Steiner here calls a 'temple' in true Rosicrucian tradition, he calls a 'building', a modern term, during the Christmas Foundation Meeting. However, the underlying truth is the same. Since then every member of the Anthroposophical Society who has lodged the Foundation Stone in the depths of his heart can participate in building the spiritual temple which Rudolf Steiner has placed as potential in the spiritual world adjoining the earth.

I have elsewhere already described in detail how every initiate who has achieved a certain stage of initiation builds a temple in the spiritual world.[105] It is important to note that in the Mystery Dramas the building of such a spiritual temple is precisely characterized by Benedictus, who also indicates that this new temple has to replace the old Rosicrucian temple. In the first Mystery Drama Benedictus describes the supersensible 'holy place' erected by him as 'my temple'.[106]

The laying of the Foundation Stone as path of initiation

To understand who this temple was built for, one has to understand the following. If we look at the esoteric background of the Christmas Foundation Meeting as a path of initiation we find the seven basic steps as described in *Occult Science* not only in the seven rhythms but also within the laying of the Foundation Stone itself. Let us now look at this from yet another angle.

As already stated, Rudolf Steiner begins the process of laying the Foundation Stone as a modern path of initiation with the stage of 'study', which means by imparting the results of his spiritual research about the three systems of the physical body in their relation to the human soul–spiritual condition. Based on this foundation of knowledge the creation of the Foundation Stone out of the macrocosm can than take place.

If we look at the reality of the Foundation Stone we notice that it first appears 'before our soul's eye' in *imaginative* form. Rudolf Steiner therefore calls it the 'imaginative form of love'. This means that if one wants to see it one has to have attained the level of imagination.

The whole event is introduced and led further by the mantric words of the Foundation Stone meditation, of which Rudolf Steiner says in the introduction to the first rhythm that it is not just spoken 'with the will of the spiritual world . . .' but that they are 'verses heard from the cosmic Word'. In the spiritual world the universal Word manifests first of all in the form of inspiration. If we want to penetrate to the source of this Foundation Stone meditation, therefore, we have to have reached the second stage of the schooling path, the stage of inspiration.

In other words, working with the Foundation Stone can lead us into the imaginative world; and the mantric words of the Foundation Stone meditation can take us into the realm of inspiration. We can say that the contents of the Foundation Stone meditation describe what one day will be apparent to the soul in the spiritual world when the Foundation Stone has been lodged in our heart and, with the aid of the mantra, has aided its development. And this is nothing less than the whole of anthroposophy, whose fundamental elements are contained in this mantra.[107]

Continuing on this path we find, in a very special way, a third, intuitive stage of higher knowledge in the laying of the Foundation Stone. In his general descriptions of the modern schooling path, Rudolf Steiner often points out that at the imaginative stage the beings of the spiritual world mainly reveal themselves in pictures; at the stage of inspiration spiritual pupils becomes aware of the deeds of these beings; and at the highest stage, that of intuition, they experience the beings themselves. In other words, they encounter them face to face. This third stage is therefore always an encounter and meeting with beings themselves.

One can likewise expect that during the laying of the Foundation Stone such a being of the spiritual world appeared and spoke directly. And this was in fact the case. The being who stands behind spiritual science and forms its inner essence, is referred to by name during the laying of the Foundation Stone. Instead of the usual term 'anthroposophy' Rudolf Steiner in his address twice uses its esoteric name and thus refers to her directly as a being of the spiritual world: 'Anthroposophia'.

The being Anthroposophia and the Christmas Foundation Meeting

This direct reference to the being Anthroposophia has a history extending over the second half of 1923—which, seen esoterically, was devoted to inner preparation of the Christmas Foundation Meeting. Rudolf Steiner delivered a cycle of eight lectures in Dornach in June, entitled: 'History and Conditions of the Anthroposophical Movement in Relationship to the Anthroposophical Society'. In his penultimate lecture, he draws members' attention for the first time to the fact that anthroposophy 'has to be acknowledged as an autonomous being' who like 'an invisible person ... walks amongst visible people ... and towards whom ... one has the utmost responsibility' and 'whom one must consult to see how she views each action we take in life.'[108]

The New Community

According to Rudolf Steiner, these three steps:

- viewing anthroposophy as a supersensible being,
- feeling the utmost responsibility towards her, and
- consulting her about one's actions, to see what she thinks of them,

are amongst the most important 'life conditions' (ibid.) of the Anthroposophical Society.

And how important this was for Rudolf Steiner can be seen from his words at the end of this cycle: 'An anthroposophical movement can only live within an Anthroposophical Society which is a reality'. Directly following this comment he explains what this 'reality' means: 'Everything has to be taken very seriously. In every moment of one's life one has to feel that one is connected to the invisible being of Anthroposophia.'[109] In this sense this cycle sets out the decisive requirement, arising out of real self-contemplation, for the anthroposophical movement in its relationship to the Anthroposophical Society.

The second big step on this path took place during the founding of the Dutch Society in The Hague in November of the same year. For this event Rudolf Steiner held a cycle of five lectures entitled *Supersensible Man*. Considering that in the above-mentioned lecture in Dornach Rudolf Steiner calls the being Anthroposophia an 'invisible human being' it comes as no surprise when at the end of his last lecture he again directly refers to her and describes her as 'living universal being ... knocking at the gates of our hearts ... saying: Let me in because I am you, I am your true human beingness!'[110] Comparing these words with those spoken earlier in Dornach it becomes clear how at first the being Anthroposophia still lives outside us so that we have to maintain a more external relationship with her, based on inner responsibility and the questions put to her. Now, in the Hague lectures this being comes much nearer to the human being as a reflection of himself, and asks to be let in through the gates of the heart.

The third step then takes place at the laying of the Foundation Stone, where she can finally enter the human heart and is therefore called for the first time by her spiritual name, *Anthroposophia*. And now Rudolf Steiner emphasizes the need for everybody to 'fill their heart with Anthroposophia'. In other words he is here concerned with the consequences of this entry into human hearts, which brings about an inner enlivening. The heart has to be enlivened through Anthroposophia before the supersensible Foundation Stone can be implanted in it.

The direct connections can be gathered from the following. In the Hague Rudolf Steiner says that entry of Anthroposophia into the human heart 'brings us true human love through what she is herself'. And the Foundation Stone of the Christmas Foundation Meeting is constituted by the substance of such love. Or, in other words, only someone whose relationship with the being Anthroposophia can ignite love in his heart towards fellow members of the Society is able to place the Foundation Stone of love within his heart. During the laying of the Foundation Stone, therefore, Rudolf Steiner says:

> And the right ground into which we must today place the Foundation Stone, this ground is our hearts in their harmonious cooperation, in their love-steeped good will to bear into the world the united anthroposophical will.

At the same time this also points to the foundation and goal of the Anthroposophical Society, in so far as it is based on the Foundation Stone.

Rudolf Steiner's pointer to *who* it actually was who time and again repeated the threefold call 'Soul of Man!', can also tell us that the being Anthroposophia, working out of the spiritual world, was directly and actively involved during the Christmas Foundation Meeting. In the introduction to the first rhythm Rudolf Steiner says that this call comes from 'the soul of man calling itself'. Recalling the lectures in the Hague where the being Anthroposophia says of herself: 'I am you; I am your true human beingness' we can understand the threefold call of the Foundation Stone as the call of 'true human beingness' within us, which we have allowed into our heart; or, which is the same thing, Anthroposophia herself.

New community

The threefold process of taking hold of the being Anthroposophia in our heart is a very inner and personal process, which can only be undertaken in complete freedom. No other being apart from the human I can allow Anthroposophia into the heart or implant the Foundation Stone afterwards. But because the Christmas Foundation Meeting was the founding of a new human community, Rudolf Steiner turns towards this supersensible being again at the end of the laying of the Foundation Stone, and now points to the central esoteric task of this newly founded Anthroposophical Society. 'Listen, my dear friends, to the sound in your own hearts'—referring to the words of the Foundation Stone meditation, which begins thrice with the call 'Soul of Man!'—'and you will here find a true union between the human being and Anthroposophia.'

From a social perspective this also shows what it means for the Anthroposophical Society to assure complete openness whilst maintaining true esotericism. The latter however, consists of the conscious cooperation of the human being with spiritual beings. In order to realize this goal the General Anthroposophical Society was founded at the Christmas Foundation Meeting so that a social temple or a social building for the being Anthroposophia could be erected on earth. And this task is sealed in the Foundation Stone meditation with the threefold call: 'May Human Beings Hear It!'

The methodological root of anthroposophy thus becomes visible. It is always founded on the freedom of the individual, the cognitive human ego, so as then to bring into community and social reality the fruits of individual development which also bear importance for spiritual beings.

Human ideal and religion of the Gods

The Bible tells us how, at the beginning of earth evolution, the heavenly Sophia built a heavenly home with seven columns. 'The wisdom built its house and their seven columns to hew' (Songs of Solomon 9,1). From the very beginning this deed stands in the spiritual world as archetype for sevenfold human development. During the Christmas Foundation Meeting however, the foundation was laid for the building which can today be founded on human freedom, and which on earth corresponds to this archetype of the heavenly Sophia.

The Foundation Stone of the Christmas Foundation Meeting can be understood as a spiritual foundation for the social building of a new soul community, enshrined in the words of the Foundation Stone meditation, which describe this highest ideal of human evolution. And according to Rudolf Steiner this is the ultimate aim of the religion of the Gods in the spiritual world.

> The aim of the creative activity of the Gods is the ideal human being ... which does not really come to life in physical man as he is at present, but in the noblest spiritual and soul life possible through the perfect evolution and training of aptitudes which this physical man has within him ... and on the far shore of divine existence there rises before the Gods the temple which presents the image of divine being in the form of the human being, as the highest divine work of art.[111]

In the same lecture Rudolf Steiner also calls this 'religion of the Gods' the 'temple of humanity' and the 'high ideal of humanity', and thus points to its *social* dimension. This is why the Rosicrucians, whose inner striving is today integrated and continued by anthroposophists, saw their spiritual and social goal in the work on the 'great temple of humanity'.[112]

It is not difficult to recognize the connection between these religions of the Gods and the Foundation Stone meditation. In its threefold uniting of the microcosmic and macrocosmic parts, it describes how human beings, right into their physical appearance, will in future increasingly become the soul-spiritual image of the highest Gods. This will not only affect individual human beings but collectively all of humanity as the tenth hierarchy.

In harmony with the seven columns of Sophia's heavenly house or temple, the seven rhythms of the Christmas Foundation Meeting represent the inner path on which every single human being *and* the human community as a whole can approach, through spiritual knowledge, the high ideal described in the Foundation Stone meditation. As once the heavenly Sophia built her heavenly house for all humanity, so in our time all those who unite freely in a new community may, through mutual collaboration, erect the soul-spiritual building on earth for their precursor and herald, the being Anthroposophia.[113] Today this can be a response to the call of the being that permeates the whole Christmas Foundation Meeting.

We can recognize the Mystery impulse of the Christmas Foundation Meeting in this powerful perspective also through its social implications. The goals have been shown to us and the ways to its realization opened.

The future of the impulse of the Christmas Foundation Meeting, and with it that of the Anthroposophical Society, lies in the hands of its members.

3. The Spirit of the Goetheanum

The esoteric structure of the Anthroposophical Society[114]

From the very beginning of his anthroposophical work, when he was still General Secretary of the German Section of the Theosophical Society—which was founded in the autumn of 1902—Rudolf Steiner took great care to shape and nurture anthroposophical work in groups. Besides devising the modern path of schooling in a way appropriate to our times, this was his most important task in the early years of the development of the anthroposophical movement.

These two aspects of his activity are closely linked. The task of the schooling path is to take hold of our higher ego. Depending on individual karma, this path may take more than one incarnation. There are also other ways to approach the higher ego. It can happen when people work together spiritually out of their common karma. If that is the case then they may experience something of their higher ego 'indirectly':

> Only indirectly does the human being experience something of his ego: that is, when he comes into relation with other people and his karma comes into play. When we meet another person and something connected with our karma takes place between us, then some impulse of our true ego enters into us.[115]

This is the esoteric reason why inner development today has to be linked to the forming of human communities. On his many travels, firstly in Central Europe, thereafter also further afield, Rudolf Steiner therefore encouraged the founding of separate local groups where anthroposophical wisdom would be nurtured. Many of these he inaugurated personally. Later, particularly during 1923, Rudolf Steiner visited a number of European countries and gave the groups there ideas about how to start a national Society.[116]

At Christmas 1923 all members and branch representatives as well as national Societies and their councils were invited to Dornach, for the purpose of calling into being there the world Society with the name 'General Anthroposophical Society'. Just as the national Societies arose organically out of the co-operation and uniting of separate local groups, so the world Society was born from the co-operation and mutual encouragement of the different national Societies. During the Christmas Foundation Meeting, Rudolf Steiner pointed to this organic emergence of the General Anthroposophical Society out of the connections formed between the national Societies: 'The suggestion had been made by me to found national Societies on the basis of which the General Anthroposophical Society would be founded here at Christmas.'[117]

Thus from the very beginning, besides encouraging the personal development of his pupils as set out in the book *Knowledge of the Higher Worlds*, it was Rudolf Steiner's aim to erect the social 'building' (in earlier lectures also called spiritual 'temple') of the Anthroposophical Society. During the Christmas Foundation Meeting Rudolf Steiner spoke about the 'spiritual Goetheanum' which was to be erected by the members of the newly founded society: 'Above all a spiritual Goetheanum must exist here as soon as is in any way possible.'[118] Besides the many suggestions for a person's individual development, anthroposophy bears a responsibility characteristic of the prevailing spirit of the time, which can only be fulfilled *in cooperative work* by separate groups of people. And one of the most important tasks was expressed in this way by Rudolf Steiner: 'Here it can only be said that people must work together with the Gods, with Michael himself.'[119]

As I have already discussed in detail elsewhere,[120] the social structure of the Anthroposophical Society can be characterized from a spiritual point of view as follows. In the groups exists the possibility to strive towards an ever more conscious cooperation with the hierarchy of the angeloi. This means creating a conscious relationship—as a reversed cultus[121]—with an angelic being, who then may become a new group soul for these anthroposophists.

Similarly, through collaboration in the different groups, a national Society can arise whose esoteric task is the search for a conscious connection to its folk spirit and, in an overall sense, a connection to the new group souls at the level of the archangels. In the present epoch of freedom, folk spirits can only fulfil their manifold tasks for humanity with the aid of human beings.

Finally, during the Christmas Foundation Meeting, a world Society was founded out of the shared forces of the different national Societies. Its task is to represent humanity before today's leading Michaelic time spirit, and cooperate with the other beings of the hierarchy of archai who are connected with Michael in the spiritual world.

Thus this Society founded at the Christmas Foundation Meeting encompasses all three ranks of beings of the third hierarchy: angeloi, archangeloi and archai—with whom, as guiding 'soul-spirits', we must today learn to cooperate in a Michaelic sense.

Only when members of the Anthroposophical Society embrace this task consciously, and sufficiently fulfil it, is spiritualization of modern earthly culture possible.

The spiritual Goetheanum as social structure

Taking the threefold structure of the Society as a basis for examining the inner nature of the first Goetheanum, we can find in it the same spiritual principle of structure. In the rainbow-like paintings of the two cupolas we find the presence of the angels, who are also called spirits of twilight and who have the task of creating the splendour of colour at the frontier between light and darkness, and pouring it into the world as from a chalice. In a different form, and even more enriched by the coloured shadows, this is expressed in the first building by the play of light and colour in the glass windows.

In the motifs of the architraves, and in particular in the capital of the great hall, the creative acts of the archangels come to the fore. Rudolf Steiner was thus able to link the seven motifs of the capitals with the essential qualities of the different nations and therefore also their folk spirits.[122] The greater spiritual force of the archangels also enables them to have a wider impact on the world of living forms and their metamorphoses.

Finally the archai give everything a firm spiritual foundation on which the first Goetheanum is to stand as a spiritual-social structure, or as the new temple of humanity. They link the being of the building with the whole of human evolution. During the laying of its foundation stone on 20 September 1913, Rudolf Steiner pointed to this: 'Let us try for a moment to think ... how the mission whose symbol this building is to become will rank in the great mission of humanity on our earthly planet.'[123] In their overlapping of two circles in the floor plan, the foundations of the first Goetheanum reveal the same archetypal idea, involving the necessary collaboration between microcosm and macrocosm, i.e. between the human world and the world of the hierarchies. This, however, is only possible through the impulse arising from the Mystery of Golgotha, which is based on the shape of a cross.

If you add seven roses to this cross,[124] you will find in the space of the great cupola fourfold man (four roses) and in the space of the smaller one his threefold higher members (three roses), which today still remain in the lap of the beings of the third hierarchy: spirit self with the angels, life spirit with the archangels and spirit man with the archai.[125]

The whole of sevenfold man in his relationship with the soul spirits—the third hierarchy—is mysteriously represented in the first Goetheanum so that we learn to build, in cooperation with the Gods, the spiritual Goetheanum between human beings as a social structure of the future. This task also corresponds to the aims of true Rosicrucianism. (See on the next page the floor plan of the first Goetheanum with the Cross and the seven roses in Christian Hitsch's drawing, made during his Easter lecture of 20.4.2003 at the Goetheanum.)

The pink South window of the great hall of the Goetheanum shows the motif 'The building becomes man' in which, through the act of Christ (central motif) the building (left motif) becomes a human countenance (right motif). On Rudolf Steiner's original sketches for the motifs he wrote: 'The threshold is veiled' and 'The threshold is revealed.' We are therefore here confronted with the mystery of the threshold to the world of the hierarchies, particularly those nearest to the human being. The beings of the third hierarchy are intimated on both the side windows.

In the lecture of 26 October 1918, Rudolf Steiner describes the new faculties humanity will develop in future. The first two already have to be present in our fifth post-Atlantean epoch. The first is to

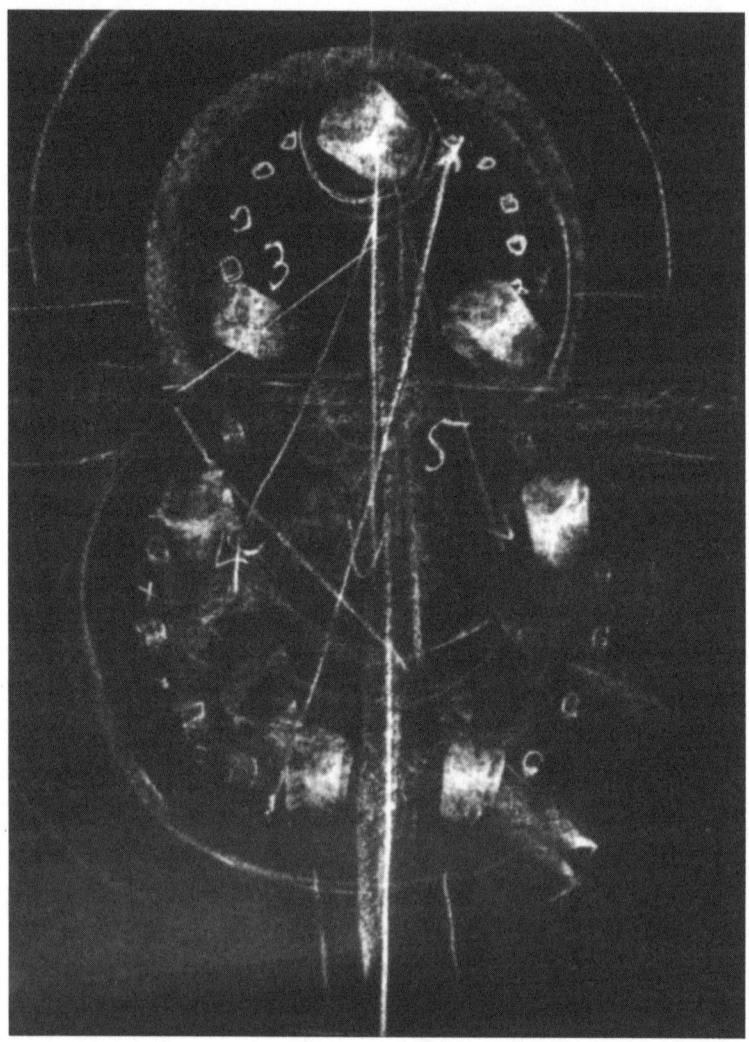

experience the human being imaginatively. 'This must come to humanity in the present age of the spiritual soul: the faculty to perceive human beings pictorially....We must learn to see through the pictorial nature of the human being to his spiritual archetype.[126] In the same lecture Rudolf Steiner also says that this faculty will lead to a real 'recognition of the ego' of our fellow human beings.

The path to develop this faculty was to be mainly through the arts because 'all art contains something that is suitable to lead us to a deeper, more tangible knowledge of the human being'. It is the arts, therefore, which 'enable us ... to understand the human being in his pictorial nature'. Rudolf Steiner spoke these words at the First Goetheanum so that the listeners could experience them at the same time as connecting with the building that as a whole represented the structure of the human being in artistic, pictorial form.

The second faculty that humanity has to develop in this epoch, at least in its rudiments (and this will continue into the next epoch) is perception of a person's relationship with the third hierarchy. This will entail us feeling through our encounter with someone his relationship to the third hierarchy: to the angeloi, archangeloi and archai.[127] For this too, the first building was to show the way. Particularly the spiritualization of language was to play an important part. This is why Rudolf Steiner called the First Goetheanum the 'House of Language' and characterized its forms as 'speech organs of the Gods'.[128] The forms and colours of this temple of humanity were to strengthen and enliven the human being's connection with the third hierarchy.

Let us also remember that the Goetheanum was received into the ether cosmos through the flames of the fire, and that Rudolf Steiner received it back from there[129] in order for it to be present at the Christmas Foundation Meeting as the 'spirit of the Goetheanum'.[130] Then we can understand even better the connection between this spirit and the third hierarchy and the task of working with it ever more consciously.

The creative force of love

From what was said earlier it is apparent that Rudolf Steiner linked the manifestation of the being Anthroposophia in 1923 with the three levels of the Anthroposophical Society which we have described. He spoke of her as 'invisible human being' in Dornach during an event organized by the local *branch group* in June. In November in The Hague during the inauguration of the *national Society* he already calls her a 'living universal being'. And during the Christmas Foundation Meeting at the founding of the *world Society* he twice calls her 'Anthroposophia', the being for whom this Society is to provide a new soul-spiritual sheath.[131]

Humanity's social sphere can only flourish through the being of spiritual love. This motif in the above-mentioned lectures therefore also required a threefold development. In the June cycle it is only indirectly mentioned. Here it is important, however, to avoid *imposing* true brotherhood and general love of mankind as a dogmatic duty on humanity, as happened with the statutes of the Theosophical Society. Rudolf Steiner says: 'If Anthroposophy itself is seen as a living, supersensible, invisible being amongst anthroposophists', in such a way that every anthroposophist follows this 'invisible being Anthroposophia'[132] then everything else that is needed for social collaboration and shared accomplishments will come about of itself.

In the Hague, however, where it is no longer a matter of small groups but of a national Society, Rudolf Steiner speaks much more directly about the shaping social impulse of this being, which lies in the awakening of the force of spiritual love. The characteristic of this 'world being' is the ability to illumine love within the heart if we allow it to enter us. Anthroposophy wishes to 'bring us—to ourselves ... and thus to that within us ... which then finds the path to others in true human love'.[133]

The final and concluding step is taken during the Christmas Foundation Meeting at the founding of the world Society. Here we not only find the revelation of love but love itself compressed into 'creative substance', from which Rudolf Steiner then forms the supersensible Foundation Stone of love.[134]

Looking at the development of this threefold love through the social stages of groups and national Societies to the founding of the world Society, which reaches a kind of culmination in the direct invocation of the being Anthroposophia, one can also experience this process as a gradual unveiling of this high being as the modern Isis. This is what wants to work today as life-giving source, not just in the sphere of the individual but also, especially, within humanity's social evolution.

In his report on the Christmas Foundation Meeting in the 'News for members' dated 3 January 1924, Rudolf Steiner writes:

> She [Anthroposophia] opens her well, and the love-borne human will can drink from it. [Only human love can approach this well of world love]. She enlivens human love and thus becomes creative in impulses of moral acts and real social life.[135]

In the Statutes too, which were made public for the first time in the same report, it says under §3 that the fruits of anthroposophy ... 'can lead to ... a social life genuinely built on brotherly love'.[136]

This describes in a more exoteric way what was realized during the Christmas Foundation Meeting in the esoteric creation of the *Foundation Stone of love* for the Anthroposophical Society. And thus it was given a perpetual spiritual source for its social structure and renewal, from which it can repeatedly draw new strength.

The new consciousness of the threshold

In 1923 Rudolf Steiner links the Hague motif of the being Anthroposophia, who knocks on the heart's door of anthroposophists, with the motif of humanity which, since the 19th century, is on the way to unconsciously crossing the threshold to the spiritual world. Both processes are linked, but this connection can only be grasped with heart thinking or heart consciousness.

On this side of the threshold anthroposophy is at first taken up through the forces of the head, as it is initially only a teaching of the contents of the spiritual world poured into earthly thoughts. From beyond the threshold anthroposophy is something completely different. There it is a real being belonging to the higher hierarchies.[137] However, one can only experience such a supersensible being by consciously entering a space beyond the threshold; that is to say, when one gains an understanding of the reality that humanity today has already passed the threshold to the spiritual world. This is also the fundamental difference between head- and heart thinking. The former remains attached only to this side of the threshold; through the latter however, we can today already awaken beyond the threshold.

Rudolf Steiner describes this in the Hague lecture that is concerned with the relationship of the human being to the being Anthroposophia: 'But whilst we have this ordinary consciousness in our heads, our deeper consciousness which touches our heart crosses the threshold into the spiritual world as a historically new step for modern civilization.'[138]

How crucial this awakening beyond the threshold is for the future, follows from the words spoken immediately afterwards: 'And beyond it humanity has either to wither or to move with good will towards a consciousness of the supersensible world.'[139]

In this critical situation for humanity today, every anthroposophist may ask himself how he can reach the experience of awakening beyond the threshold. The answer according to the lecture mentioned above is by experiencing Anthroposophia as a real spiritual being permitted to enter our hearts, so as to there develop in us a new sense organ for our collaboration with the beings of the third hierarchy. Then the living being Anthroposophia will, from beyond the threshold, lead local groups to work with the angeloi, the national Societies to work with the archangeloi and the world Society with the archai, with Michael himself. And so the above-mentioned task will be fulfilled, which lies in the cooperation between man and Gods.

Based on this, we can rightly understand the inner relationship between the spirit of the Goetheanum, which has returned from cosmic heights, and the being Anthroposophia. In the light of this spirit—her being constituted of human beings with angelic hierarchies—increasingly emerges after the fire until, at the Christmas Foundation Meeting, she is revealed in her full cosmic glory to humanity, which is then able to create 'a true union ... for Anthroposophia' in the threefold configuration of the Anthroposophical Society we have described.

To make possible such a union of human with spiritual beings in the social sphere too, Rudolf Steiner first had to bring the spirit of the Goetheanum down to the earth. This he describes at the end of the Easter cycle in 1924:

> Henceforth [after the burning of the Goetheanum] we understand that we can no longer merely represent an earthly concern, but we represent a concern of the wide ethereal universe wherein the spirit lives. For the concern of the Goetheanum is indeed a concern of the wide-spreading ether wherein there dwells the spirit-filled wisdom of the world. It has been borne forth and we may now fill ourselves with the Goetheanum impulses as with impulses coming towards us from the cosmos.[140]

From these words it follows that, because Rudolf Steiner was able to be 'permeated' during the Christmas Foundation Meeting with the impulses of the cosmic spirit of the Goetheanum, it is now active on earth from the region of the 'spirit-filled *wisdom*' or the sphere of Sophia, with which the being Anthroposophia is also connected.[141]

On the last day of the Christmas Foundation Meeting, Rudolf Steiner describes how fully this spirit of the Goetheanum was present during it: 'I knew I had permission to say what occurred here because it was said with full responsibility before the spirit who is and will be the spirit of the Goetheanum.'[142] Thus the Mysteries of the new Isis-Sophia could be unveiled within the spiritual Goetheanum's temple and become the beginning of conscious collaboration between humanity and Anthroposophia, who after the Christmas Foundation Meeting, as true supersensible being, permeated even the least actions of the newly founded Anthroposophical Society with her presence. Now, in harmony with the spiritually resurrected Goetheanum, she was able to work right down into social relationships, thus creating the new community between humanity and the third hierarchy.

4. Working with the New Group Souls

The new group souls

In his lecture on 1 June 1908, Rudolf Steiner speaks of how today group souls await earthly human beings in the spiritual worlds. In contrast to previous group souls, these take full account of human individuality and the attainment of freedom—which is why Rudolf Steiner calls them *new* group souls.

It seems obvious that these new group souls belong to the *third* hierarchy, because only such beings can directly guide human groups (the second hierarchy works primarily through nature, and the first through world processes). Rudolf Steiner describes their characteristics as follows: 'All former group souls were beings who made people unfree. These new beings, however, are compatible with complete freedom, and the preservation of human individuality.'[143]

This characterization begs the question of where these new group souls learned how to engage with freedom in a way that now enables them to act upon it—in contrast to the old group souls, who were not able to do this. This obviously stems from the fact that they were able to experience something of the being of freedom in the spiritual world during specific moments of their own development.

In order to understand how this is possible, it is good to remember how Rudolf Steiner differentiates between earthly and cosmic freedom. The former is described in his book *The Philosophy of Freedom*; and of the latter he says: '*The Philosophy of Freedom* prepares us to recognize through freedom what can then be experienced through spiritual union with Michael.'[144] Only through the latter can the 'cosmic being of freedom' be recognized.[145] This 'cosmic freedom' is thus intrinsically linked with the being and deeds of Michael working out of his cosmic sphere of the sun.

Thus Rudolf Steiner calls Michael the 'spiritual hero of freedom',[146] whose aim it is 'that man be a free being'.[147] Union with him in the spiritual world is described in the karma lectures. There it is shown how the spiritual Michael path leads to his supersensible school in the sun sphere. Rudolf Steiner says of this school that there, amongst other things, the contents of all pre-Christian mysteries were lifted from the sentient soul and the intellectual soul into the consciousness soul by those human beings who participated in it during their life between death and a new birth.[148] This highest member of the human soul is also the only means to actually grasp and experience the essence of freedom. This means that here, in the sphere of cosmic freedom, the purpose or new faculty of freedom was implanted in the human being so that later, on earth, he might grasp the essence of human freedom as outlined in *The Philosophy of Freedom*. The supersensible school of Michael was thus dedicated to developing freedom.

Rudolf Steiner also mentions that numerous elemental spirits participated in this sun school alongside human souls: in particular all three beings of the third hierarchy, i.e. those angeloi, archangeloi and archai who belong to the cosmic kingdom of Michael and who serve him:

> All the discarnate souls belonging to Michael took part in this great school in the supersensible world during the 14th, 15th and 16th centuries. All the beings of the hierarchy of angels, archangels and archai who belonged to the Michael stream, as well as many elemental beings, participated in it.[149]

To better understand Michael's relationship with the being of freedom, it is important to be clear about where his supersensible school is located in the cosmos. According to Rudolf Steiner, the spiritual sun in our universe is the source of cosmic freedom. He speaks of this in almost hymn-like words:

> Thus in our whole world existence our humanness is linked to sun existence and we can feel, addressing the sun: O universal son of freedom, I feel your relationship to everything within me that gives my own being freedom and resolve for the future![150]

In another lecture he says: 'And the sun existence is working whenever you are conscious of freedom of choice.'[151]

Michael is the great ruler of the cosmic sun sphere. He is the most advanced of the hierarchical beings guiding humanity because, in contrast to the other archangels of his rank, he represents a star, the sun, rather than a planet. And this difference is precisely the important thing. All planets absorb spiritual impulses from without, but the sun emanates them, sending its light into the whole universe—whereas the planets can only reflect it. Rudolf Steiner says of him: 'But the highest in rank, as it were the chief, is the one who takes over the leadership in our age—Michael.'[152] Therefore his spiritual inspirations relate to those of other archangels 'as the sun to the planets'.[153] 'Michael is as superior to his companions as the sun is to the planets.'[154]

As the chief representative of the sun sphere, Michael acts in the spiritual world as the great representative and teacher of cosmic freedom, which is directly related to the central spirit of the sun—the Christ being, whom he serves and whose countenance he is within the cosmos. Therefore his supersensible school is located where the foundations have been laid for a new cosmic Christianity, which has to become a Christianity of freedom. And the human souls who were later to become the souls of anthroposophists on earth were karmically guided to this Michael school in the sun sphere during their life after death. In their earlier incarnations they were already able to absorb the Christ impulse in such a way that a longing took root in their hearts to experience Christ's cosmic dimension. 'Karma has so guided these souls that in the life between death and a new birth they thronged at that time around Michael, preparing to carry down a cosmic Christianity again to the earth.'[155]

Elsewhere Rudolf Steiner says the following about the relationship of humanity—quite unusually addressing it as hierarchy[156]—and the beings of the third hierarchy with the Christ and his sacrifice on earth:

> Thus we see that for the beings of these four hierarchies—not only for the human being, but also for angels, archangels and archai—the Christ event signifies the very highest experience of which we can speak in our cosmic evolution.[157]

And because Rudolf Steiner spoke previously of how *these* angels, archangels and archai had already absorbed the Christ impulse, it follows that human beings, who are here placed in a direct, even 'hierarchical' relationship with them, also belong to those who have found a deeper relationship to Christ—first on earth in their former incarnations and then, during the joint founding and development of a new cosmic Christianity in the Michael school.

Here we have to ask the following: Is it not so that a number of angels, archangels and even archai found their way at that time into the supersensible Michael school out of similar motives, i.e. through their relationship with Christ; and with the task thus acknowledged of thoroughly acquainting themselves with the essence of cosmic freedom which emanates from him, so as to then guide humanity in accordance with this freedom? In various places Rudolf Steiner states that such beings of the *third* hierarchy—who had already absorbed the Christ impulse in the spiritual world so as to lead humanity on earth in harmony with Christ through the fifth (angel), sixth (archangel) and seventh (archai) cultural epochs—did indeed exist.[158]

It therefore seems justified to think that especially *these* hierarchical beings participated in the Michael school in order to learn from him things about the nature of freedom which they would then be able to use so as to unite, as new group souls, with human communities on earth in the new and totally free way described, thus predisposing humanity for its re-ascent into the spiritual world, and also actually beginning this.[159]

The reappearance of the Christ, and the third hierarchy

In his essay *The Spiritual Guidance of the Individual* Rudolf Steiner points out that in our time especially, the angels who during the fifth post-Atlantean epoch guide us in harmony with the Christ, also inspire anthroposophy on earth.

> And if nowadays anthroposophy is cultivated, this constitutes recognition of the fact that the super-human beings who formerly guided humanity are now continuing their task as leaders in such a way as to be themselves under the direct guidance of the Christ. Thus it is with other beings also.[160]

Here 'super-human beings' are the angels; and 'other beings' refers to the archangels and archai following the Christ.

We know from the karma lectures that, in the supersensible school on the sun, Michael himself was preparing anthroposophy in its still heavenly form in union with the angels, archangels and archai serving him. And when Rudolf Steiner says that anthroposophy is 'our gift from Michael'[161] who is now the leading time spirit and who works here on earth with humanity through those beings of the third hierarchy connected to him, then we have further proof that these are the same beings of the third hierarchy who once participated in the supersensible school under the leadership of Michael together with discarnate human souls, and had previously grasped the Christ impulse particularly strongly.

In the same essay Rudolf Steiner goes on to say that it is the same angels today who lead mankind to experience Christ in the etheric: 'So also in the 20th century it will be these same teachers who will lead human beings to behold the Christ as Paul beheld Him.'[162] This suggests that today, especially, anthroposophy has the global mission of preparing humanity for this encounter with the etheric Christ, for it is the same angel beings who today inspire anthroposophy and prepare Christ's reappearance in the etheric. And the cosmic source of these two tasks lies in the Michael school from which they draw the forces to fulfil this dual mission. If we understand this then we also understand the importance of the following words by Rudolf Steiner: 'We thus comprehend spiritual science in a completely different sense. We learn that it imposes a tremendous responsibility upon us, since it is a preparation for the quite specific and tangible reappearance of Christ.'[163]

However, the Mystery of this being is still more profound. Just as today the angels connected with Michael-Christ lead humanity to the reappearance of Christ in the etheric, so during the sixth epoch the archangels connected with him will lead humanity to His next, still higher manifestation, where Christ will appear in the astral in the lower devachan. And later still, during the seventh cultural epoch, the archai will prepare humanity for an even greater revelation: as universal ego in higher devachan.

> The Christ individuality was on earth in the body of Jesus of Nazareth for only three years and will not come again in a physical body. In the fifth post-Atlantean epoch He will come in an etheric body, in the sixth, in an astral body, and in the seventh,

in a mighty cosmic ego that will be like a great group soul of humanity.[164]

In another lecture, Rudolf Steiner says of this third supersensible revelation of Christ that humanity will then perceive Him 'in His glory, as the form of the greatest "Ego", as the spiritualized Ego-Self, as the great teacher of human evolution in the higher devachan'.[165]

The cosmic meaning of these increasingly profound revelations of Christ can be seen from a brief remark Rudolf Steiner makes in his book *The Spiritual Guidance of the Individual*. In Chapter 3 he writes that the angels who today lead humanity to perceive Christ in the etheric also show us 'how the Christ not only works upon the earth, but how He spiritualizes the whole solar system'. This means that what was spiritually laid down within the earth at the Mystery of Golgotha as the new sun,[166] has, through the etheric appearance of the Christ, today extended its force throughout the solar system. If we trace this process further then the might and glory of Christ at his appearance in the lower devachan will stretch as far as the zodiac or the world of the fixed stars. (According to Rudolf Steiner's spiritual-scientific research the world of the stars already lies in the upper region of lower devachan.)[167] At his third and hitherto highest revelation from higher devachan, Christ will reveal Himself as the all-encompassing universal ego or 'in His true ego that surpasses all human egos in inconceivable greatness'.[168]

At this stage the force of Christ's cosmic ego will ray towards humanity without any sheath, directly from the sphere lying on the far side of the zodiac. Then Rudolf Steiner's words will be fulfilled: 'In the future, people's hearts will be filled with a Christ idea whose magnitude will surpass anything humanity has known and understood so far.'[169]

And as today the Michaelic angels lead mankind to an experience of the etheric Christ, so the Michaelic archangels and Michaelic archai will lead mankind towards even higher revelations of the Christ. 'Thus, step by step, humanity is led into the spiritual world.'[170]

That these beings of the third hierarchy will be first and foremost those who have a special relationship to Michael and who partook in his supersensible school, follows from the fact that he himself took part in the Mystery of Golgotha and, more than any other hierarchical spiritual being, can therefore pass on this knowledge to other spiritual beings. 'Michael himself, in the supersensible worlds, has participated in the results of the Mystery of Golgotha.'[171] 'For him the Mystery of Golgotha signifies the transformation from a spirit of night into a spirit of day.'[172] In other words he moves from the cosmic countenance of Jahweh to the cosmic countenance of Christ. Thus for the third hierarchy he gradually became the great teacher of the Mystery of Golgotha. At the same time, as the cosmic countenance of Christ and, particularly after assuming leadership of humanity as time spirit, he is the one who stands closest to Him.

This is why Rudolf Steiner writes of 'Michael-Christ' as the one who leads humanity towards 'its universal goals',[173] which will be achieved primarily with the aid of the third hierarchy. And of Michael's relationship with the etheric reappearance of Christ, Rudolf Steiner says: 'This event, the appearance of Christ ... can only be brought about by the ever-spreading rulership of Michael.'[174]

In this expansion of Michael's rule in the spiritual world participate chiefly those angels, archangels and archai who passed through his supersensible school in order to recognize the Christ impulse in its Michaelic form and to serve it under the leadership of Michael.

What is already taking place in spiritual regions therefore has to continue on earth in complete freedom. For this to happen, however, conscious cooperation between humanity and the new group souls belonging to the Michaelic beings of the third hierarchy is necessary. They and the human souls were both prepared for this in the supersensible school of Michael; and during the Christmas Foundation Meeting the Anthroposophical Society was founded as the place where the first steps towards accomplishing this task could be taken.

Sun karma of anthroposophists

Before his lecture of 23 May 1924 in Paris, Rudolf Steiner looked back to the Christmas Foundation Meeting and spoke of a new alliance that he had been able to form with the spiritual world: 'But the hope remains that the strength of our alliance with the good spiritual powers, which we were permitted to form at the Christmas Foundation Meeting, ... will be able ... to defeat all adversarial forces in the spiritual realm.'[175] The Michaelic picture of the fight with the dragon clearly lives in these words so that one can identify Michael and the angels, archangels and archai from his supersensible school as the 'good spiritual powers'.

During 1924 Rudolf Steiner took great pleasure in repeatedly saying to members in various places: 'It may now be said that ever since the new foundation of the Anthroposophical Society at the Goetheanum last Christmas, those spiritual powers from whom our revelations are received have showered upon us even greater grace than before.'[176]

The relationship with Michael and those hierarchies connected to him therefore became still more intense after the Christmas Foundation Meeting. And since Rudolf Steiner built this bridge, it continues to be the task of humanity to *freely* reach out to the outstretched arms of Michael and his servant.[177] Only in mutual freedom can this new relationship with the spiritual world be developed. Implicit in this is the kind of freedom whose foundation Michael himself and the group souls of the third hierarchy connected with him once laid down for humanity.

This also points to the cosmic place where the new group souls and humanity are able to learn about freedom: the *supersensible school of Michael*. And this means that a special karma has been formed between these new group souls and the souls of anthroposophists, because of what they experienced there *together*. From then on they have been mutually dependant, needing each other in order to fulfil the cosmic-telluric task given by Michael himself. This has to happen at all three levels: with the angels at the level of local groups, with the archangels at the level of national Societies, and with the archai belonging to the school of Michael and the leading time spirit Michael at the level of the world Society.

What was created as disposition in the sun sphere has to be freely fulfilled on earth as the creation of new, future karma between mankind and these three types of hierarchical beings. This is why Rudolf Steiner founded the Anthroposophical Society at the Christmas Foundation Meeting and gave it the threefold form that has been described, which corresponds to the nature and work of the third hierarchy.

Nowadays one repeatedly hears anthroposophists saying that the structure of the Society is no longer appropriate. Depending on the nature of the difficulties they experience, they speak either of local groups, national Societies or even the world Society as being outmoded. This opinion, however, can only be justified from *this side* of the threshold. From *beyond* the threshold the situation looks completely different. Seen from there the work with all three types of new group souls is one of the most important tasks that anthroposophy must accomplish in the social realm.[178]

Rudolf Steiner says of such collaboration with the new group souls: 'The more that connections are formed where feelings of fellowship develop in complete freedom, the more will lofty beings descend and the more rapidly will the earth planet be spiritualized.'[179] In other words, the greater the network of human connections formed by people on earth through anthroposophical groups, national Societies and the world Society, the more will the higher group souls be able to unite with them in free cooperation: the angels with the groups, the archangels with the national Societies and the force of the archai with the world Society.[180]

Thus, by working together, humanity will form soul-spiritual vessels on earth for the higher beings, in full accord with the true Grail Mystery of the present. And this will accomplish the first important step towards the 'highest ideal of human evolution', towards 'spiritualizing the earth planet', of which Rudolf Steiner writes at the end of his *Occult Science*: 'We see then that "knowledge of the Grail" culminates in the highest imaginable ideal of human evolution—that of spiritualization brought about by the human being's own efforts.'[181] This puts into the proper cosmic-telluric perspective the most important social task which we as anthroposophists have brought to earth from the Michael School—that of serving Michael by collaborating with the spirits of the third hierarchy. It could also be said that a kind of spiritual agreement has been reached with the new group souls. And the most important characteristic of the Anthroposophical Society as a new karmic community lies in the fact that within it not only human karma but also the karma between humanity and the hierarchical beings can develop in complete freedom, in concord with the Christ who is the guardian of karma.

The new group souls and the Foundation Stone

In the aforementioned lecture of 1 June 1908, Rudolf Steiner also points out that this cooperation between humanity and the new group souls can be strengthened if 'humanity freely allows its feelings'—not just its thinking—'to stream together' so as to 'group ... around centres'. For 'the feelings, which thus flow together *into a centre* now cause beings to work together like a kind of group soul.' But in contrast to the old group souls, these 'new beings' ... are now in harmony with the complete freedom and preservation of human individuality.'[182]

This points towards a future ideal that today can be achieved on earth only by very few, highly developed individuals, whom Rudolf Steiner calls 'masters of wisdom and *harmony of feelings*' and of whom he says that they are 'directly connected with the forces of the higher hierarchies.'[183] What these masters have already done, many human beings, following their example, now have to develop *between one another,* so that a new bridge between the spiritual world and humanity can gradually be built in the social sphere.

If we look in more detail at the esoteric structure of the Anthroposophical Society that has already been mentioned, then the importance of the spiritual Foundation Stone given at the Christmas Foundation Meeting will become ever clearer to us. If humanity has really implanted this in its heart, where it becomes the spiritual basis for a new community, then human beings can also direct towards this 'centre' the highest feelings of soul, which they develop through anthroposophy and in particular through group work. Then a person's feelings will meet and flow together with similar feelings of other members of the group, who have also planted the Foundation Stone in their hearts; and from this a strong, united centre of feeling arises. This then forms the source of strength, which Rudolf Steiner described as follows during the Christmas Foundation Meeting:

> The proper soil into which we must place this Foundation Stone today consists of our hearts in their harmonious collaboration, in their good, love-filled desire to work together to carry the will of anthroposophy into and through the world.[184]

This *Foundation Stone of love* can only be nurtured in human hearts based on the feeling of selfless and thus harmonizing love, which unites with the substance of love of the Foundation Stone and gradually fills the whole soul.

Then humanity will increasingly understand how this Foundation Stone can mediate between human beings and the new group souls. Its threefold structure is what primarily contributes to this. Through the development of spiritualized human thoughts within the soul, the human being will encounter the universal thoughts of the angels in the essence of the Foundation Stone; through the creation of free human imagination he will become aware of the universal imagination of the archangels; and through the increasing development of spiritualized human love, he will experience the universal love of the archai and in particular the cosmic love of Michael himself.[185]

This threefold relationship between human beings and the beings of the third hierarchy—which also forms the threefold structure of the Anthroposophical Society—is indeed possible through the Foundation Stone if only members can focus their spiritual feelings on it in complete freedom, as the unshakeable foundation for their collaboration with the new group souls.[186] This is why, immediately after the ceremonial laying of the Foundation Stone, Rudolf Steiner so forcefully urged those present: 'Let us remain aware of this Foundation Stone of the Anthroposophical Society, formed today. Let us remember it in all that we shall do, in the outer world and here, to further, to develop and to fully unfold the Anthroposophical Society.'[187] As has already been shown this is only possible, from an esoteric perspective, with the aid and cooperation of the new group souls of the third hierarchy.

However, if the spiritually uniting essence of the Foundation Stone is neglected by the Society, and if more and more disputes and divisions arise, then what Rudolf Steiner warns of will occur: 'The more that people are divided, the fewer lofty souls will descend into the human sphere.'[188] This means that when disagreements and divisions amongst anthroposophists occur at the level of local groups, the latter become disconnected from the angels; if such divisions spread into national Societies, these will grow disconnected from the archangels; and if discord and divisions take root in the life of the world Society then even the archai, and in particular Michael, will no longer be able to descend into it. And because our relationship with these beings of the third hierarchy was karmically predisposed in the Michael School, anthroposophists become karmically disloyal to their own Michaelic karma through such a failing in relation to the core social and esoteric task of the Anthroposophical Society—with all the consequences arising from this for themselves and the development of all humanity. Thus today we stand at the beginning of a time when it 'lie[s] in the souls of human beings themselves whether or not they give as many as possible of such higher souls the opportunity of descending.'[189] In other words, the new group souls are here and they await our answer, which we can only give them out of our common endeavour in realizing anthroposophy as social impetus. In the epoch of freedom however, the hierarchies are increasingly dependent on human beings. They can only work amongst humanity when we truly want it, thus enabling the higher spirits to do their work.

This is why, in the Michael School on the sun, Michael himself already brought the souls of future anthroposophists into a relationship with these spirits of the third hierarchy, so that the karmic foundations could be established for initiating a future collaboration between the Gods and humanity on earth.

★

Finally, I wish to address a different question. Lately I have been asked whether Rudolf Steiner really founded the new Mysteries during the Christmas Foundation Meeting, or whether this was just a 'renewal' of the Mysteries in general.

Here one has to note that although Rudolf Steiner really founded the new Mysteries during the Christmas Foundation Meeting, he did not refer to this fact in his lectures and addresses to the members of the Anthroposophical Society, but unexpectedly to the founding circle of the Christian Community. Thus, in the third lecture of the Apocalypse cycle, he said to the priests: 'We have characterized what can make the Christian Community the bearer of an important part of the new Mysteries.'[190]

These words clearly testify to the fact that for Rudolf Steiner the Christmas Foundation Meeting, and therefore also the new School of

Spiritual Science, were about the *new* Christian Mysteries. These have to be nurtured with a certain intensity particularly within the Anthroposophical Society and in the 'soul' of the free School,[191] so that the priests of the Christian Community are also able to better understand and take up *their own* esoteric task on that basis. In order to understand 'part' of the new Mysteries one first has to come to understand 'the whole'. For this to be possible, Rudolf Steiner admitted all the founding priests into the First Class of the esoteric school. He wanted to help them fulfil their 'essential part' within the new Mysteries by having a consciousness of the whole.

However, this first has to live within the Anthroposophical Society so strongly that the various 'parts' of the new Mysteries really receive their nourishment and inner support from this central spiritual source.[192] In consequence the members of the Anthroposophical Society can learn what responsibility they bear for the future of the new Christian–Michaelic Mysteries on earth.

5. The Christmas Foundation Meeting and the Mystery of the Resurrection

We brought the Meeting to a formal conclusion, but actually it should never be closed; it should continue perpetually in the life of the Anthroposophical Society.
(Rudolf Steiner, 6 February 1924)

The Christmas Foundation Meeting of 1923/24, when the General Anthroposophical Society was founded, rightly counts as a highpoint in Rudolf Steiner's biography, and likewise in the development of anthroposophy on earth in general. From a historical aspect this event falls in the 21st year of anthroposophy's earthly development, and thus comes as the full revelation of its spiritual being (the manifestation of the forces of its 'ego').

Rudolf Steiner himself speaks of how he had to wait for three seven-year cycles,[193] saying that the 'specifically esoteric aspect [had] to wait', so that finally, during the Christmas Foundation Meeting, he could begin carrying out his true mission of this incarnation: the founding of the new Christian Mysteries, with their direct spiritual connection to the Mystery of Golgotha. This founding of the new Christian Mysteries, however, did not only lie in conveying new esoteric wisdom, but also in a free creative deed of the spirit, one that was for the first time enacted by a human being, and the highest archetype of which lies in the resurrection of Christ Jesus at Golgotha and its consequence, the birth of the resurrection body as 'a new member of human nature'.[194]

Since that time, uniting with the forces of the resurrection body has led humanity to participate in the process of the spiritualization of the earth, as well as the gradual development of a completely new type of humanity—a divine humanity—on earth.

The Foundation Stone of love

Just as the Mystery of Golgotha was a macrocosmic event that took place on earth only once, the highpoint of modern Christian initiation is the microcosmic recurrence of this highest deed of Christ in individual, creative human deed. This is in full accord with Christ's prophetic words that one day humanity will also do 'the works that I do'. (St John 14, 12).

This is precisely what occurred during the Christmas Foundation Meeting when Rudolf Steiner drew on the highest forces of the spiritual world to create the 'Foundation Stone of love', and laid it as foundation for the General Anthroposophical Society. This direct connection of the Christmas Foundation Meeting with the nature of the Mystery of Golgotha enabled him to call it a 'cosmic turning point of time'.

The substance of love, of which the Foundation Stone was created, points to its further task as basis for a new cosmos of love in the spiritual world, which will one day develop out of the present cosmos of wisdom—as Rudolf Steiner writes in his book *Occult Science*. In the last chapters of the Apocalypse this future cosmos of love is presented as a great imagination of the 'New Jerusalem'. Rudolf Steiner created a foundation stone for it during the Christmas Foundation Meeting. And after handing it to humanity he gave us the possibility of participating in this process of creating a new cosmos.

The Foundation Stone meditation

The Foundation Stone meditation is inseparably linked to the Foundation Stone. Working with it and its rhythms spiritually can help a modern human being to find, on the path of self-knowledge, the spiritual core of his own being, his true ego, and through this a new relationship with Christ as the 'universal I' who represents the highest archetype of the individual ego of every human being. In addition, this inner work with the meditation can lead to a conscious experience of Christ's presence and efficacy in one's soul. Alongside receiving the forces of the resurrection body and participating in building a new cosmos, this is one of the major tasks of the new Christian Mysteries.

Thus the three main aims of these Mysteries are:

- Experiencing the Christ in one's own soul as the divine 'I am' and the highest archetype of the human ego (our immortal individuality);

- Absorbing the forces of the resurrection body and developing a divine humanity;
- Transforming the earth into the dwelling place for the new cosmos of love. The participation of humanity in building the 'Heavenly Jerusalem'.

The Christmas Foundation Meeting

We can discern three basic themes in the Christmas Foundation Meeting:[195] Every day began with an esoteric part followed by detailed discussion and adoption of the statutes of the General Anthroposophical Society. During the evenings Rudolf Steiner gave a cycle of nine lectures entitled 'World History Illuminated by Anthroposophy as the Foundation for Knowledge of the Human Spirit.'[196]

The meetings held every morning during these eight days predominantly belong to the actual esoteric contents of the Christmas Foundation Meeting and can be divided into three parts:

- Creation of the Foundation Stone by Rudolf Steiner during the morning of 25 December 1923;
- The first speaking of the Foundation Stone meditation (same day), which, if worked on inwardly can lead us to experience the Foundation Stone in the sphere adjoining the earth, and thereafter to implanting it in our own heart;
- The rhythms of the Foundation Stone meditation; inner work with them can lead to a strengthening and further development of the Foundation Stone within the human soul.

The process of creating the Foundation Stone as esoteric core of the whole of the Christmas Foundation Meeting can also be seen in three parts:

- At the level of knowledge Rudolf Steiner presents the threefold archetype of the earthly human being;
- At the level of creativity the Foundation Stone was created out of the forces of the Holy Trinity as a supersensible reality;
- At the final, social level, the Foundation Stone meditation was given to the members of the Anthroposophical Society as its spiritual foundation.

Since then, every member of the Anthroposophical Society has had the possibility of laying the Foundation Stone in his heart, where it can become a link between humanity and the resurrection body as the spiritual core of the Mystery of Golgotha and the source of all creative forces of the future cosmos.

The Anthroposophical Society

As is clear from Rudolf Steiner's comments, a Foundation Stone can only be laid down in the heart as a free decision arising from individual efforts. However, once this has been done, this Foundation Stone works within the heart as a sustaining basis for the human community which Rudolf Steiner called the General Anthroposophical Society. Then it becomes the spiritual foundation of this new community, whose task is to develop the new Christian Mysteries on earth, drawing the impulse for this from the forces of the time spirit. This, in turn, is the sunlike 'countenance of Christ'—the archangel who leads and guides humanity today—Michael.

If members of the Anthroposophical Society follow Rudolf Steiner's directions and lay down the Foundation Stone in their hearts, basing all their anthroposophical deeds unshakeably upon this foundation, the Anthroposophical Society will become what its founder described at the end of the Christmas Foundation Meeting: 'a strong, shining'[197] Society that fulfils its tasks in the world in concord with Christ and Michael.

Anthroposophists can be guided on this path by the supersensible being 'Anthroposophia' who, as the contemporary messenger and herald of the heavenly Sophia, was invisibly present at the Christmas Foundation Meeting, illuminating it from beginning to end.[198] It is for this reason that Rudolf Steiner twice turned to her directly during the laying of the Foundation Stone, calling her by her spiritual name of 'Anthroposophia'.

Thus Rudolf Steiner accomplished the Christmas Foundation Meeting under the overlighting presence of those three beings who inspired the whole of the anthroposophical movement from the beginning: Christ, Sophia and Michael.

Appendix 1
The Esoteric Background to Electronic Media

Understand[ing] sub-nature for what it really is.
Rudolf Steiner, March 1925[199]

Introductory remarks

The reader of this work may ask how this appendix relates to the themes so far discussed. The answer to this lies in the last chapter, which shows that the search for a spiritual relationship with Rudolf Steiner and his most important esoteric deed on earth—the Christmas Foundation Meeting as foundation for the Anthroposophical Society—can become the spiritual means to create a necessary counterbalance to computers and the internet, and the publication of Rudolf Steiner's esoteric texts in electronic form.

Esoteric dimensions of the internet

The nature of the internet is best understood esoterically on the basis of Rudolf Steiner's Dornach lecture of 13 May 1921.[200] In this lecture Rudolf Steiner describes how the further development of today's abstract intellect will slowly produce a new kind of natural kingdom. This intellect, which is merely of a 'shadowlike character' can only function 'automatically'. It can only comprehend matter as such, and never the etheric. Even less can it penetrate the soul or spirit world. This ghostly natural kingdom will be formed between the mineral and the plant kingdom, and will come to life following the reunion of the moon with the earth in the 7th to 8th millennium.

The imagination of the spider web

It is alarming how accurate Rudolf Steiner's descriptions of this ghostly realm appear in relation to the contemporary world situation:

> And from the earth will arise a terrible race of beings, in character midway between the mineral and plant kingdoms, as robotic beings of extreme, intense and logical intellect. They will spread and take hold of the earth, overlaying it as with a web of terrible spiders—spiders of enormous wisdom, whose organization does not however even reach the level of plants. These terrible spiders will interweave and intermesh with each other, imitating in their movements all that human beings have conceived with their shadowy intellect—without allowing it to be inspired by a new imagination, and all that is to come through spiritual science. All unreal human thoughts of this kind will assume the reality of being. The earth will be covered [...] with terrible, mineral-plant-type spiders, which will spin very rational interconnections with each other but with malevolent intention. And the human being [...] will have to merge his being with these terrible mineral-plant spider creatures.[201]

These spider creatures will be distinctly ahrimanic in character. Reading these prophetic words of the spiritual scientist today, in an era of global computer and internet links, you may feel disheartened to realize how quickly this prophecy is becoming a reality on earth. It is as if Rudolf Steiner, with his spiritual gaze, was describing today's internet from beyond the threshold, categorically warning humanity that in a not too-distant future, when moon and earth reunite, this whole internet and computer web—and in fact everything connected with the development of the artificial intellect—will suddenly come alive. And then we 'will have to merge [our] being with these terrible mineral-plant spider creatures.' If one considers how many, particularly young people, have become computer addicts and spend most of their time in front of the screen without sufficient will to relinquish it, then one can imagine the nature of this endlessly greater dependency on such a spider kingdom if this whole web comes to life in future. It will be well-nigh impossible to disconnect ourselves from it. The alarming picture of an insect caught in the net of a huge and ravenous spider, trying in vain to free itself, offers an appropriate picture of this human future. And it will be a very special task of white magic to free such people from their bond to these beings.

Created with intent

In the above-mentioned lecture, Rudolf Steiner also indicates that there are certain occult circles well aware of this approaching danger, and intent on advancing it by deliberately keeping this secret. 'There are those [human beings] who are quite *consciously* allies of the intention to enmesh human existence.'[202]

If we take Rudolf Steiner's words seriously, there can be no doubt that precisely these occult circles, which know of the above-mentioned secrets and yet push humanity further in this forlorn direction, also coined a fitting name for the internet, the most appropriate instrument for achieving this future, and have spread it like a secret code: www—World Wide Web.

In my view these occult circles belong to the secret fraternities of the English-speaking world whose occult-political endeavours Rudolf Steiner characterized in such an illuminating way in his lectures during the First World War.[203] That does not mean however, that those who gave the internet its name themselves belong to these occult circles. They are more likely to be standing at the margins and being used without their knowledge. This begs the question whether some of the other tags used in the world arise from the same source, for instance the 'Sorat' hotel chain in Germany (whose biggest hotel is in the centre of Berlin); or the satellite aerials which display in big red letters the name 'SatAn' at the centre of their dish; or the latest computer systems in which one finds demonic pictures and words—as for example the internet browser 'Mozilla' portraying the head of a red dragon etc.[204] At the end of the same lecture Rudolf Steiner reiterates, as if in anticipation of criticisms from some anthroposophists: 'Humanity may close its eyes to such things, and may say: Well, this is reading too much into it. But the signs are really there and human beings should understand the signs.'[205] Such signs, which can be seen clearly today and must be understood, in particular by anthroposophists, also include the following.

The number of the Beast

According to the occult teachings of the Kabala, all Hebrew letters have a numerical equivalent. Rudolf Steiner spoke about this in detail in his cycle on the Apocalypse in relation to deciphering the name of the sun demon 'Sorat'.[206] On this occasion Rudolf Steiner points out that the numeric equivalent of the letter *W* (Hebrew waw) is the number 6. It follows that the occult meaning of 'www' is '666', the number of the beast, of which the Apocalypse says: 'Here wisdom itself speaks. Whoever has the ability to think it, let him seek the meaning of the number of the beast. It is the number of Man. And its number is six hundred and sixty-six.'[207] The 'number of Man' means that the beast, which is not of human nature, will use something derived from man himself for his attacks against humanity. In my opinion the internet and everything connected with artificial intelligence are part of this.

In conclusion, the aims of the above-mentioned occult circles not only relate to the spiritual enmeshing and entrapment of humanity, but ultimately to placing the whole undertaking at the service of 'Sorat'. Because the latter is primarily the opponent of the ego-principle within humanity, the enmeshing of humanity by an artificial intelligence that has come to life must ultimately lead to loss of the ego.

Connecting to sub-nature

It is clear that today's digital industry is being driven precisely in this direction. At present computers are still based on silicon chips, which are used predominantly to carry electricity and store information. But the next generation of chips is just around the corner, in which not only electricity but also light will be used as information carrier. This means that a chip of the same size can contain infinitely more information. But this is still a long way from the end-goal of development in this field, as there are already big companies in the West experimenting with chips no longer based on light but on microbiological elements as information carriers. These new 'biological chips' will again substantially increase the units of information they can hold compared to 'light chips'. Because they will be permeated by electricity, these biochips will doubtless be firmly bound to sub-nature from the start. Thus the whole development is unmistakably moving towards Rudolf Steiner's imagination of a spider web criss-crossing the earth, and later coming to life.

Electronically compressed

Something similar, although in a different form, occurs in the case of the CD, DVD or external Hard Disc Drive. To understand what this actually means we have to remember that when the cosmic intelligence overseen by Michael descended from the sun to the earth in order to become human intelligence there,[208] it underwent a massive process of compression or contraction. This intelligence, where Ahriman does not seize hold of it in the human being, repeatedly becomes 'naturally' free again after death during the expansion of the ether body into the cosmos—that is, during the process which forms the polarity to its previous compression. Only the modern path of schooling, founded on the development of living thinking, can already bring about this expansion into the spiritual world during earthly life, and hence ensure humanity's new, conscious connection with the cosmos, and there with Michael himself.

Particularly since 1998 (3 × 666), the ahrimanic powers serving Sorat have been working in opposition to this.[209] Ahriman—making use of the forces of sub-nature—wants to penetrate Michaelic intelligence with his artificially created intelligence, which includes the digitalization of thought. For him this is one of the ways in which he can gain power over earthly intelligence. It began with the fixing of human thoughts through printing technology and now continues with its digitalization. 'What does Ahriman intend to gain from Michael through print? He wants—and you can see it happening everywhere today—to conquer intelligence: this conquest of intelligence will take hold wherever conditions are favourable.'[210]

And Ahriman finds these favourable conditions especially in the world of the computer and digital industry.

Anthroposophical material

With the digitalization of Rudolf Steiner's work, the largest complete edition on earth, the process of ahrimanic 'compression' is palpable. The entire collection of Rudolf Steiner's works today encompasses nearly 350 volumes. Digitally collated on CD-ROM this still means a fair number of discs. With the latest DVD technology, however, all

350 volumes can be compressed onto two or three discs. On hard disk drive there will be sufficient space left for the whole artistic legacy. If one has some feeling for a spiritual perspective, just thinking about this almost gives rise to physical pain.

At the same time this incredible fixation and compression of spiritual material is accomplished because the CD-, DVD- and computer industry drag everything even further into sub-nature—in contrast to print which, although it too has already been claimed by Ahriman, has been and to a certain degree still is connected to the natural world via its mechanical processes. In sub-nature, however, the ahrimanic forces possess extraordinary powers with which they will devise even greater technical 'miracles' in future than has been the case so far. Do not succumb to the illusion that it is possible to 'ennoble' the internet or CD/DVD in the way Rudolf Steiner implied for printing. In the realm of sub-nature, obstacles are greater by far. One of the reasons for this is what Rudolf Steiner states as one of the main conditions for the ennoblement of print: 'We have to redeem print through reverent feeling for what lives in Michaelic wisdom.'[211] In contrast, the internet, DVD or HDD reduce everything to the level of purely abstract information and, in addition, cut everything up into tiny, byte-sized fragments (which recalls the image of Osiris cut into pieces by Typhon) thus spreading it amongst humanity in a way that makes 'reverent feeling' impossible.

The delusion of the binary system

If one inquires into the nature of the computer on this basis, examining the way information is processed and stored, then one discovers that everything is based on the binary system (zero or one, yes or no, true or false), which can be multiplied endlessly and quantitatively through repetition and different combinations. Rudolf Steiner calls this fundamental principle, which forms the basis for computers across the world, the 'delusion of the binary system'.[212] This also connects directly to the power within humanity that in our time fights most ardently against the Michaelic impulse, the latter always being connected with the number 'three': 'In this new consciousness of humanity is contained the delusion of the binary system, which veils the truth of the number three.'²¹³ After this passage, Rudolf Steiner goes on to describe how everything arising from Michaelic inspiration is always threefold: the threefold social order, the three figures in the Representative of Man, the rhythm of the Foundation Stone meditation. Here the Anthroposophical Society and in particular the School of Spiritual Science have a special task: to consciously oppose the ahrimanic principle of the binary system, which computers in particular have spread across the world, with the threefold Michaelic principle as the most important foundation stone for a future spiritual culture; and to realize it in all areas of human life and activity.

Ahriman's incarnation

In the same lecture Rudolf Steiner speaks further of the duad or binary number: 'Everything that is active in this illusory conception is the creation of the ahrimanic influence, of that influence which in the future will concentrate in the incarnation of Ahriman of which I have already spoken.'²¹⁴ It follows that the whole computer- and internet industry is today the most effective way to prepare for the imminent incarnation of Ahriman, or at least to allow his earthly task to run as smoothly as possible. The 'inter-net', the worldwide web of ahrimanic spider beings enmeshing the earth, will from the outset have a direct relationship to Ahriman's physical appearance on earth: it will serve him particularly effectively, and offer extremely favourable conditions for his activity.

Today one can already find on the internet the most vindictive and defamatory attacks against Rudolf Steiner, anthroposophy, Waldorf schools and other institutions and offshoot movements connected with anthroposophy. And this global spread and adverse impact go far beyond that of print. There is no doubt that this will increase in future, particularly with the publication of the complete edition on the internet and DVD, because then all alleged 'vulnerable passages' will be easily and quickly accessible.

Living with the computer

What has been said does not mean, however, that one should refrain from using a computer or the internet. They are part of our civilization. At the same time they represent the greatest ahrimanic temptation which humanity faces today, and will have to face increasingly in the future. It is crucial, however, as with many similar problems we face in contemporary civilization, that *we* control the computer and the internet, rather than *vice versa*. The reverse can easily occur if we do not take seriously or ignore Rudolf Steiner's advice and therefore do not realize what is actually happening. If we want to maintain our autonomy in relation to the computer world, we have to differentiate between using an objective, purely technical aid in our work, and overstepping the mark so that, at first unnoticeably, ahrimanic seduction starts to take control. In the latter instance we increasingly start to become an instrument for alien purposes, without being aware of it, and slowly slip into sub-nature ourselves.[215]

Reading in the astral light

In his lecture of 13 January 1924, Rudolf Steiner pointed to the most important ahrimanic impulses of the present: everything connected with heredity, all forms of nationalism, mechanical, merely word-based thinking, and finally the way we deal with script. The latter in particular can effectively impair the development of our capacity to read in the astral light, and thus to draw near to Michael. Rudolf Steiner mentions here that in certain Rosicrucian schools learning to write was prohibited until the age of 14 or 15 so as not to spoil children's higher spiritual capacities. For the same reason letters are first taught in Waldorf schools through painting and drawing, before progressing to reading.

Print with its ahrimanic tendencies was inspired by the sub-earthly 'ahrimanic counter-school' opposed to that of Michael: 'Although the art of printing has to be seen as a spiritual force, it is one which Ahriman has established in opposition to Michael.'[216] You will notice that this ahrimanic tendency finds its continuation, if not indeed its culmination, in today's digital forms of print in order to achieve its aim even more effectively: that of cutting human beings off from their ability to read in the astral light and thus to encounter Michael in the spiritual world.

The new imaginations

That the internet not only stands in polarity to the sphere of Michael in the spiritual world but that it is its ahrimanic counterpart, can be seen from Rudolf Steiner's description of cosmic intelligence: 'Intelligence is the way in which the higher hierarchies govern their mutual conduct and encounter. What they do, how they interrelate, how they are with each other, that is cosmic intelligence.'[217] The internet is increasingly assuming a similar function among human beings. Here, in purely ahrimanic form, the attempt is made to create a worldwide web that connects as many people as possible—but in such a way that humanity becomes increasingly sundered from the cosmos and the hierarchies, and is thus bound up with what was described above as an ahrimanic spider web. Michaelic intelligence came to earth from the spiritual world so that human beings can achieve freedom through insight. Addiction to the computer, however, leads to the exact opposite.

Through the continued sundering of human beings from the spiritual world, the 'human intellect will become increasingly shadowy'.[218] This process is particularly reinforced by the global spread of the computer. To counteract this one has to integrate the 'new imaginations' of spiritual science with today's 'shadowy concepts and intellectual ideas'.[219] Yet by imprinting their contents onto DVD or HDD the precise opposite occurs. As purely intellectual 'information' on the worldwide web, the living imaginations of anthroposophy are being incarcerated in an occult prison.

The special nature of the Class texts

The publication on HDD of the class texts (as well as of rituals and other esoteric texts by Rudolf Steiner) can be experienced as particularly tragic. Rudolf Steiner makes a particularly clear distinction between the contents of the Class and his other esoteric lectures. The latter are given to humanity as thoughts and ideas, and from the very beginning therefore seem as if enclosed in a protecting sheath. (This is why Rudolf Steiner was able to agree to general publication after the Christmas Foundation Meeting.)

It is a different matter with the contents of the Class lessons. Here we have a substance, which comes directly from Michael himself (from the Michael school) thus retaining its original, imaginative forms, which require a totally different approach. Rudolf Steiner points to this character of the Class contents as follows:

> Generally it will therefore have to be the case that a person gets to know the spiritual world first of all in the form of ideas. It is in this way that spiritual science is nurtured initially within the General Anthroposophical Society. However, there will be individuals who wish to participate in the representations of the spiritual world which ascend from the form of ideas to expressions which are adopted from the spiritual world itself. [...] For these individuals there will be three classes of the 'School'. Here the studies will ascend to an ever higher degree of esoteric insight. The 'School' will lead the participant into the realms of the spiritual world which are not accessible in the form of ideas. Here it becomes necessary to find a means of expression for imagination, inspiration and intuition.[220]

Hence the way we treat the Class contents has to be fundamentally different from how we approach the more general contents of Rudolf Steiner's lectures. He quite clearly demanded a different relationship to the contents of the Class than was required in approaching his published lectures.

Dangers and tasks

During a private conversation Rudolf Steiner once indicated that the greatest future danger to anthroposophy would be its increasing intellectualization, thus putting it into the hands of Ahriman, the lord of death.[221] The publication of Rudolf Steiner's complete works on the internet and HDD brings this increased danger of intellectualization ever closer, and with it a further step towards the fragmentation of anthroposophy.

This process has to be countered by an increased and conscious intensification of esoteric work within the School of Spiritual Science, as well as meticulous study, which avoids intellectualism, of Rudolf Steiner's texts. He expected his pupils to work with his texts in a particular way: not with the abstract and increasingly shadowy intellect, but with the 'hearts' which, in the Michaelic sense 'start to have thoughts',[222] and therefore enable us to ascend to true imaginations. Only by this means can a place be created within the human being himself where anthroposophical wisdom is protected from Sorat and the ahrimanic powers serving him. Such care for anthroposophy could be a primary task for all groups within the Anthroposophical Society.

The necessary counter-balance

The pervasiveness of computers amongst humanity today is assuming breathtaking dimensions. Because of increasing computerization, also in China, India and South America, this development is advancing inexorably, and taking all before it. The computer is increasingly replacing cinemas (also for viewing video or DVD) and television. Much points to the fact that computers equipped with light- and later even with biochips (see above) will increasingly replace all other forms of media and eventually eradicate them.

The following words of Rudolf Steiner, which in their day primarily related to film and cinema, are today also relevant for computers: 'Many phenomena of cultural life today have a destructive effect, especially screen images—which definitely harm the etheric body. Such images also arouse sensuality.' And directly after this Rudolf Steiner points out what can help humanity: a true art inspired by the spiritual world and spiritual science, which gives the necessary inner strength even when the soul is pervaded by electronic media.

> True art can bring down into the sensory world what comes from higher worlds. In the science of the spirit we work together with supersensible powers. Spirit knowledge is the only thing that gives us inner certainty ... Only our own inner, wakeful activity can give the soul certainty. A spiritual-scientific attitude sustains people and makes them happy, for what the science of the spirit gives offers them a solid point of reference in their inner lives, as necessary to the soul as daily bread to the body.[223]

Materialism reinforced by the globally expanding computer network spreads the creation of a 'virtual reality' in which human beings unconsciously try to take refuge from the materialism encircling them.

More and more people spend their time in the world of shadows and boundless dreams in order to escape otherwise tormenting problems and questions. This however increasingly unleashes the wildest human desires. Rudolf Steiner points to this danger: 'This extends from the dreams of drunken people right through to the mad urge to commit crimes, for the adversaries of the archai work in this way into the sense world.'[224] This is the work of ahrimanic beings who today revolt against the Michaelic time spirit and who resort to all means possible. Today this includes the computer and internet.

Unfortunately it will be impossible to stop or evade this development:

> Each person must try to sense his place in the world, must experience something of what is storming into humanity in the way that has been described. Weakness, uncertainty, loss of equilibrium will otherwise become the rule. People who swing between fantasy and materialism will never find their way.[225]

Therefore—and this has to be stressed again in all clarity—it is not a matter of retreating in alarm from computers and the internet or abstaining from them. What we should do instead is not become euphoric or obsessed with the technical possibilities offered by the internet or computers, which can escalate into downright addiction, but create an appropriate counterbalance in the spirit to what is a necessary development in the material realm.[226]

In particular three negative consequences for human beings of the world of computers and its wider application (also as photographic image producer) have to be pointed out. They are:

- Passivity in the thinking realm;
- Destruction of the faculty of imagination; and
- Weakening of the will.

All these bear a distinctly anti-Michaelic character. This can be seen clearly from the following. Michael, the 'fiery Prince of thought in the universe'[227] expects humanity to use its freely endowed intelligence to actively penetrate the spiritual world with understanding, so that a conscious relationship with Michael and the spiritual sphere can develop.

Michael is also directly involved in the process beginning in our time in which 'gradually the force of imagination will enter into the common intellectual consciousness of humanity'.[228] The most important task of the remaining centuries of the fifth post-Atlantean epoch is the decisive step of grasping hold of conscious imagination, through which humanity can consciously enter the spiritual kingdom where today the etheric Christ lives.

Michael also has an important task to fulfil today in relation to the human will:

> It is the task of Michael to lead man back again, on paths of will, to where he came from when he descended on the paths of thought from the living experience of the supersensible to experience of the sense world with his earthly consciousness.[229]

In other words, Michael wants to lead humanity back in a new, conscious way, upon the paths of will that primarily involve the will within thinking, from the sense-perceptible realm to an experience of the supersensible.

From what has been said it is clear that the three forms of debility of the inner human being resulting from excessive preoccupation with electronic media, have a decidedly anti-Michaelic character. It is therefore vital to counteract this with appropriate spiritual-scientific measures, which have their source in Michael himself, in order to combat the ahrimanic attack on humanity from the sphere of sub-nature.

> In the science of the spirit we now create another sphere in which there is no ahrimanic element. And precisely by taking up this spirituality of knowledge to which the ahrimanic powers have no access, the human being is strengthened to confront Ahriman *within the world*.[230]

Intensive spiritual-scientific study, practised with greatest earnestness as taught in the first stage of the modern path of initiation, is needed to counteract the widespread passivity of thinking.

> One has to get used to seeing things as they are in the world, from great, selfless points of view. The best way of doing this for an

ordinary person wanting to follow the Rosicrucian way is to study the elementary things taught by the science of the spirit... Working with these truths cleanses one's thinking and disciplines it, so that one is then ready for the steps in occult training that follow.[231]

In relation to this, Rudolf Steiner points in particular to his books *Truth and Science* and *The Philosophy of Freedom*, and calls the study of and preoccupation with them a 'mental and spiritual exercise' in thinking. Thus spiritual science can give humanity the tool to overcome passivity in thinking, which is a disease of our civilization.

Through electronic media, human thinking becomes increasingly dependent on the forces of *sub-nature*, even if this is an unconscious process for most people. This demands a conscious correction of thinking, a counterbalance from *super-nature:* in other words, thinking focused on the contents of the spiritual world. This can be achieved through the careful study of spiritual science.

The same goes for the dimension of imagination. Photographic images (cinema) deaden the forces of the soul's imagination but this can be counteracted especially by 'real art', which finds its impetus in the higher worlds. For this, however, we need to develop in the direction of real heart thinking. In contrast to the head, the human heart thinks in imaginations, which can then exert a constructive, enhancing social effect, which in turn can overcome the solitude and loneliness caused by computers.

Here it must be emphasized, however, that this does not relate to art in general and also not to any kind of art, but solely to an art that enlivens and activates the human etheric body. This is found in particular in genuine eurythmy, true speech formation and artistic work with colours rooted in etheric experience. But because even these arts have already partly lost their connection with the enlivening ether forces today, strict differentiation needs to be applied in respect of this criterion.

Goethean observations of natural phenomena too, which have a strong imaginative character, develop forces which are useful for counteracting the destruction of the imagination by electronic media.

It is important to highlight once again the fundamental difference already mentioned between a text that appears on a screen and the printed page of a book. The latter, as end product, still belongs to the natural world and can therefore be artistically enhanced in many ways, principally offering the reader the possibility, based on its format, of bringing an appropriate mood to bear on the contents of the book. This, however, completely disappears with electronic reproduction of a text, as it is concerned solely with the level of 'information'.

The weakening of the will likewise, something that in our time has long become a general feature of civilization, is exacerbated by the time spent in front of the screen. Here there is a danger that people with an already weakened will force are far more easily manipulated by the above-mentioned occult circles. Through electronic media they can become an easy target for these largely unknown entities.

This real danger can only be countered by the free decision to meditate, which Rudolf Steiner calls the human being's freest deed, and which can lead to an earnest and energetic meditative life. Work on the so-called accompanying or subsidiary exercises can likewise be of great help here.[232]

It is high time that we found the inner courage through spiritual science to recognize that electronic media now, as once did the invention of printing, represent the strongest weapons against Michael. The latter however was still created from natural forces whilst the latter rise up from sub-nature.

The opposing orientations of the electronic media and the Michael impulse can be highlighted by two further examples. Rudolf Steiner says of Michael: 'He liberates thought from the sphere of the head; he clears the way for it to the heart.'[233] Exactly the opposite happens through the electronic media, where thought is cemented strongly into the head region. Here the danger arises that the heart forces increasingly become subject to stronger impulses from sub-nature and the realm of instinct. The path of the dragon from the sub-conscious regions of human will, which are connected to the metabolic system, opens up in the direction of the heart. How Michaelic forces can counteract this today is described in detail by Rudolf Steiner in the lecture of 27 September 1923.[234] However, these Michaelic forces can only become effective in us when, above all, our fascination with the boundless possibilities of electronic media is replaced by a real enthusiasm for working meditatively with a spiritual content.

The second example is linked to the following words by Rudolf Steiner:

> It is Michael's mission to introduce into human etheric bodies the forces by means of which thought-shadows may regain *life*; then the souls and spirits in the supersensible worlds will incline towards these enlivened thoughts.[235]

These words show the extent to which the being of electronic media counteracts Michael. Electronic media as it were preserve the shadowy nature of human thoughts, and Virtual Reality incarcerates them in a dungeon. This makes it so much more difficult to stimulate our thoughts and take them into a conscious contact with the good beings of the spiritual world.

Study of spiritual science, an interest in genuine art and an active Michaelic meditative life can offer an effective antidote to the unavoidable encounter with electronic media in today's civilization. This makes it possible to maintain the relationship with Michael and even enables his impulses to be taken down into the realms of sub-nature.

In other words, it is not a matter of remaining passive towards the immense temptation linked to electronic media, but, as they are a reality of today's world, to take on the Michaelic fight and battle with them. For this, the right preparation and weapons are required, as discussed earlier in this chapter.

The Anthroposophical Society, and its esoteric School, can become a strong bastion against the negative global effects of electronic media. The former through intense cultivation of the study of spiritual science and advancement of various anthroposophically inspired arts; and the latter through developing an active and Michaelic meditative life that is appropriate for our times.

The second temptation, which the internet in particular spreads through humanity, is the illusion that its possibilities offer a new kind of social network between people. But here it is easy to overlook the fact that this arises only at the level of pure 'information', and only within sub-nature. Here too it is not a matter of condemning this kind

The Esoteric Background to Electronic Media 117

of connection, but more of creating a counter-balance. This can only be accomplished along the lines of the quote by Rudolf Steiner which heads this appendix, when increasing ensnarement of humanity by the forces of sub-nature is clearly recognized, so that a new, and fully conscious relationship between people, created out of free will, can arise with the help of super-nature.

At the Christmas Foundation Meeting, through the newly founded Anthroposophical Society, Rudolf Steiner established the preconditions for this kind of community-building that draws on the forces of super-nature. As mentioned elsewhere, this involved the fulfilment of Christ's words: 'My Kingdom is not of this World' (St. John 18, 36), which Rudolf Steiner interpreted as meaning that Christ Himself descended into *this* world so as to establish his own kingdom in the midst of the world controlled by Ahriman, and give humanity the possibility of participating in the development of Christ's kingdom.[236]

Moving on from this archetype, Rudolf Steiner gave the members of the Anthroposophical Society the supersensible Foundation Stone or the Foundation Stone of love, so that based upon it a new human community could arise. This community can then stand fully within modern, and largely ahrimanic civilization but is anchored in something which, as Foundation Stone of love, was not brought from this world but from the realm of Christ.

Thus Rudolf Steiner gave humanity a new and at the same time thoroughly Christian social form; and as this spreads across the world it is able, from the supersensible world, to create a counter-balance to the spider web described earlier, that rises up from sub-nature.

From what has been said it becomes clear how closely the subject of the electronic media is connected with the second part of this book. With the Mystery of the laying of the Foundation Stone, Rudolf Steiner gave humanity a spiritual tool to engage, in a Michaelic way, with much that is only just now beginning to afflict us, but undoubtedly will continue into the future.

The subject discussed at the beginning of this book is closely connected with the problems we are considering here. Whilst the electronic publication of the esoteric contents of Rudolf Steiner's work is now an unalterable reality, the question remains as to how, in this case too, we can create a counter-balance. The solution in my view lies in the task presented in the first section of this volume: How do we find a direct relationship and connection with Rudolf Steiner today?

If this relationship is established and continues to be nurtured by the members of the Anthroposophical Society then the negative consequences of such publication for the future destiny of the Michael School can be averted. Only through a real relationship with Rudolf Steiner will the condition stipulated by him, that his work is never to be separated from his name, be assured. It is not only humanity that can ensure this, but also the spiritual world, anthroposophists who have crossed the threshold into the spiritual world, and Rudolf Steiner himself.

For that to happen, however, a further condition must be fulfilled. Now that Rudolf Steiner's complete works, including the most intimate and esoteric texts, have been made available to the wider public—which is unlikely to engage differently with them than with any other esoteric literature on the market—the following is even more necessary than during Rudolf Steiner's lifetime. There must be people who bring an appropriate mood of receptiveness to bear on the content which Rudolf Steiner developed out of the nature of modern initiation, and which forms the core of the new Mysteries. Only by this means can the publication of these texts be balanced and redressed in a spiritual way, and thus the otherwise unavoidable damage avoided.

Rudolf Steiner speaks of this in the last lecture of the Easter cycle which he held after the Christmas Foundation meeting in Dornach:

> But this above all will be necessary: knowledge, vision, and conscious experience of the spiritual that can arise from modern initiation must be freely met by reverence and true respect. For if we do not revere, if we do not treasure it, true knowledge or indeed any spiritual life of humanity is in reality impossible.[237]

Today, in contrast, the electronic media in particular hold sway with singular success over everything that falls within their realm of power—so that even esoteric texts are dragged down to the level of pure information, and thus every feeling of 'reverence and true respect' is nipped in the bud.

The Esoteric Background to Electronic Media

This tendency, however, has to be countered by a conscious process that was taken up and developed by Rudolf Steiner and which goes back to Goethe, Schiller and Novalis. Goethe would never have embarked on his groundbreaking scientific studies without the capacity to approach natural phenomena with the deepest reverence. And Schiller would never have developed his revolutionary ideals of freedom without the same deep reverence for the nature of humanity. Novalis, likewise, would never have established his magical idealism without the profound reverence which he bore within him for the world of spirit.

One can therefore see in the words of Rudolf Steiner just quoted a direct link with and development of what Goethe had already referred to in the 'Pedagogical Province' of Book 2 of *Wilhelm Meister's Apprenticeship*. There he points out that no one nowadays brings the forces of veneration with him as a natural gift into the world but has to develop it freely as a task: 'But there is one thing nobody brings into the world, and yet it is on this that everything depends nevertheless if humans beings are to be fully human... Devotion!'[238] Thus Goethe was already pointing out that we can no longer draw on old, inherited forces of devotion, but on *new* ones gained through self-education.

Only when members of the Anthroposophical Society activate these forces—which, as we have seen, create the foundation of the modern schooling path in the epoch of the consciousness soul—and bring them to bear on the esoteric texts of the Michael School, can a counter-balance be achieved which redresses the publication of these texts in general, and their electronic format in particular.

These are the most urgent tasks of the Anthroposophical Society on the one hand and the School of Spiritual Science on the other. If, in the former, there is an intensified preoccupation with the Mysteries of the laying of the Foundation Stone—that is to say with its esoteric foundations—so that the fruits of such work become visible as a community-building principle; and if within the School of Michael, the relationship to its founder Rudolf Steiner and its leading time spirit is properly nurtured, then in my view the negative consequences of the above-mentioned publications can be averted.

Then the calamity—as in Goethe's fairytale—can be transformed into an even stronger impetus for our work, and into renewed will for taking hold of and fulfilling the goals that Rudolf Steiner set for the Anthroposophical Society and its soul, the free School of Spiritual Science.

Appendix 2
Rudolf Steiner on the Youth of the Future[239]

'The youth of the future comes from a completely different cosmic world than we and this will intensify. It brings with it an immense ability to think, a virtuosity of thought. But that is the greatest temptation and at the same time the greatest ahrimanic attack against anthroposophy. It will be a danger because, due to the tremendous ease with which anthroposophical concepts are grasped, things will remain in the realm of thinking, and an enormous sense of comfort will develop within anthroposophical thought; but this will not progress into self-development and schooling.

The only thing youth can be given to strengthen it to survive future events is the encounter with anthroposophical schooling. This schooling is the only foundation on which study can reach its true goal. If Anthroposophy is taught as academic subject it becomes harmful. Anthroposophy must never remain pure theory; it has to come alive. If it stays simply as teachings or doctrine it is killed off and handed to Ahriman, the master of death. But nowadays people find it much more comfortable and convenient to think, and to adopt a few anthroposophical concepts rather than to discard a single habit.

What anthroposophy does for our souls is much more important than any amount of theoretical understanding of spiritual scientific concepts.'

Notes

1. *Conversations of Goethe with Eckermann and Soret*, translated by John Oxenford, Everyman, Dent 1930.
2. Lecture of 13.1.1924. *Rosicrucianism and Modern Initiation*, Rudolf Steiner Press, London 1965.
3. *The Philosophy of Freedom*, Rudolf Steiner Press, London 1964 (translated by Michael Wilson), p. 139. Italics by Rudolf Steiner.
4. *Knowledge of the Higher Worlds and its Attainment*, Rudolf Steiner Press, London 1969. Rudolf Steiner dedicates six pages to the necessary development of and attainment of devotion.
5. That Rudolf Steiner too sometimes voiced criticism does not contradict this. Usually he preferred to characterize the issue or offer a spiritual-scientific diagnosis. He rarely spoke critically and, when he did, it was in an objective fashion, like the voice of universal justice. He only criticized where absolutely necessary, and as an initiate he could also compensate for the consequences of this in the spiritual world.
6. Lecture of 28.10.1909. *Metamorphoses of the Soul*, Rudolf Steiner Press, London 1983.
7. *Knowledge of the Higher Worlds and its Attainment*, op. cit.
8. Lecture of 20.10.1906. *Original Impulses for the Science of the Spirit*, Completion Press, Lower Beechmont 2001.
9. Lecture of 30.1.1924. *Die Konstitution der Allgemeinen Anthroposophischen Gesellschaft und der Freien Hochschule für Geisteswissenschft*. GA 260a.
10. Rudolf Steiner's words according to Ita Wegman: 'I only have to leave the physical plane and if it were then possible for the adversary forces to separate anthroposophy from me in the sense that my teachings go out into the world without knowledge of my person so that they are diffused, then what ahrimanic beings want and aim for would be accomplished' ('News for Members', 28.6.1925).
11. Ibid.
12. *The Philosophy of Freedom*, op. cit.
13. Letter of 11.8.1904, *From the History and Contents of the First Section of the Esoteric School, 1904–1914*, Anthroposophic Press, New York 1998. Italics by Rudolf Steiner.
14. Ibid., letter of 12.8.1904. Italics by Rudolf Steiner.

15. Friedrich Rittelmeyer: *Rudolf Steiner Enters My Life*, Christian Community Press, London 1963.
16. *Human and Cosmic Thought*, Rudolf Steiner Press, London 1991.
17. Taking the seven world views into account it becomes clear that even the thinking of two people can be completely different. Rudolf Steiner often points out that for example the thoughts of Vladimir Soloviev or Leo Tolstoy (particularly in his book *About Life*) are fundamentally different from the way of thinking in Central and Western Europe. Nevertheless Rudolf Steiner regards especially the former as representative of the consciousness soul.
18. See chapters 1 and 2 of this book.
19. In this essay dated 1908 Rudolf Steiner still uses the term 'Theosophy'.
20. Ibid.
21. *From The History and Contents of the First Section of the Esoteric School*, p. 227, op. cit.
22. Ibid.
23. Christoph Lindenberg, *Rudolf Steiner. Eine Biographie*, Vol. 1, Stuttgart 1996.
24. 'The Connection of Man with the Elemental World. Finland and the Kalevala', Typescript Z 144 (Rudolf Steiner Library, London).
25. It is not without significance that, according to Professor Alfred Castelliz, Slavic tribes lived in the area around Pettau—one of the larger towns near Kraljevec—as early as the Grail centuries (8th–9th centuries). The burial remains on the western side of the Schloßberg (castle mount) testify to this. Thus this area may be the only one where Slavs came into contact with the Grail Stream with which, according to Rudolf Steiner, their future would be deeply connected (see lecture of 3.11.1918 in *From Symptom to Reality in Modern History*, Rudolf Steiner Press, London 1976). Professor A. Castelliz, from whom come many of the indications used by Viktor Stracke in his essay (see below), was himself a native of the former southern Styria, and came from near Cilli. He studied architecture in Vienna and visited the first Goetheanum in Dornach. He was so impressed by it that he became one of Rudolf Steiner's pupils. Later Rudolf Steiner asked him to design the first school building and visited him during his last stay in Vienna in September 1923.
26. Marie Steiner, *Die Anthroposophie Rudolf Steiners. Gesammelte Vorworte zu Erstveröffentlichungen von Werken Rudolf Steiners*, Dornach 1967.
27. Lecture of 12.6.1910-II. *The Mission of the Individual Folk Souls in Relation to Teutonic Mythology*, Rudolf Steiner Press, London 1977.

28. I received this essay from Viktor Stracke († 29.10.1991). It constitutes the first chapter of his book *Vom Schicksalsnetz Europas. Einzelne Erscheinungen aus dem Kulturleben im Zusammenhang mit dem Ort ihres Auftretens betrachtet* (unpublished typescript in German).
29. This is a passage in Wolfram von Eschenbach's *Parsifal* where the geographical details are surprisingly exact. It is possible that he did not just stay in Aquileia, but according to A. Castelliz's research also in Castle Montpreis near the town Planina—which at some time belonged to the Templars—and whose ruins are still in existence. According to tradition a significant part of *Parsifal* was written at Castle Montpreis (particularly the ninth book). From there Wolfram would have travelled on the old Roman Road to Pettau; he could not otherwise have known of the small stream Grajena—mentioned in the epic—which is so small that not even all the inhabitants of the town (today Ptuj) know of it.
30. Around this time the knight Gandin must have owned a large estate in this area, otherwise he would not have been able to leave to his daughter Lammire all of what was then southern Styria and give Ither the land of Kukum (the area southwest of the Drau) as tenure. From the size of his land it can be assumed that he also owned the Island of Mur. A mention of the Grail stream in former southern Styria, in the ninth chapter of Wolfram's *Parsifal*, does not contradict the traditionally reputed presence of this stream in northern Spain, but points rather to its geographical spread and East-West extent.
31. This name, Mont-Sal-Wotsch or Mont-Zal-Vo—written either in a more Germanic or more Slavic way—reminds one surprisingly of Mont Salvatsch (Munsalvaesche) of the Grail Mysteries. This does not negate the fact that mountains of this name were also found throughout all the geographical locations of the Grail Mysteries (i.e. from northern Spain to Styria).
32. A question that has not been entirely resolved is the precise location of the seat of Parsifal's grandfather Gandin. On the one hand it seems logical to look for it in Haidin (linguistically connected to Gandin). This suburb of Pettau however lies on the right, on the flat banks of the Drau. During Roman times there was a camp called Petovio, as attested by many Mithrans. However, one can hardly imagine that in this flat area there would have been a castle, as on the northern bank of the Drau there is a beautiful hill overlooking the whole area, on which today stands the impressive Palace of Pettau. It is assumed that originally a Celtic Sanctum stood on this hill. The walls of today's palace rest on mighty ashlars

whose age is hard to determine, and which were uncommon during the Middle Ages. Also the stream Grajena runs into the Drau from the north, which suggests that the Gandin's family seat was on the Pettau Hill. This is where Gahmuret was born and brought up.
33. The area north of Pettau, southern Styria, was given by Gandin to Gahmuret's sister, Lammire, and the area west of Cilli later went to Ither, who married Lammire. Wolfram mentions this area as the Land of Kukumer because it lies on the River Gurk (Kukuma) which flows into the Save.
34. Albrecht von Scharfenberg describes this in his epic *Der Jüngere Titurel*.
35. Viktor Stracke quotes from a book which researches the Slavic roots of the Grail mountain 'Mont-Sal-Wotsch'. Accordingly the translation of this name is 'the great or majestic mountain, Wotsch' which in Slavic is 'Bo'.
36. *Das Geheimnis der Trinität*, GA 214.
37. Lecture of 12.6.1910-II. *The Mission of the Individual Folk Souls in Relation to Teutonic Mythology*, Rudolf Steiner Press, London 1977.
38. Lecture of 31.12.1923. *World History in the Light of Anthroposophy*, Rudolf Steiner Press, London 1997.
39. For more on the relationship between the Rosicrucians and the Grail Mystery see lecture of 24.6.1909 in *The Gospel of St. John*, Anthroposophic Press, New York 1962.
40. *Karmic Relationships Volume VI*, Rudolf Steiner Press, London 1971.
41. See M. and E. Kirchner-Bockholt, *Rudolf Steiner's Mission and Ita Wegman* (private printing). According to Viktor Stracke, Ita Wegman tried to get hold of Castle Borl for the Anthroposophical movement as she knew about its spiritual background from Rudolf Steiner.
42. It is not without significance that Rudolf Steiner spent holidays with Marie Steiner near this area (Triest/Portorose) between April and June 1911.
43. Lecture of 7.2.1913. *The Mysteries of the East and of Christianity*, Rudolf Steiner Press, London 1972.
44. See S. O. Prokofieff, *Rudolf Steiner and the Founding of the New Mysteries*, chapter 7, Temple Lodge Publishing, London 1994.
45. Ibid.
46. See also *Rosicrucian Wisdom*, Rudolf Steiner Press, London 2000.
47. *Parsifal*, Vintage Books, 1961 (translated by Helen M. Mustard and Charles E. Passage).
48. References relating to the place Poglet-Anschau are from Heinrich

Stracke's readers' letters: 'Hinweis auf das Geschlecht der "Anschau" ', *Nachrichtenblatt*, 21/2006.
49. From a lecture by the author given on 3 April 2005 at the Iona building in Driebergen (Holland).
50. For more on the relationship of anthroposophy to the book *The Philosophy of Freedom* see S. O. Prokofieff, *Anthroposophie und 'Die Philosophie der Freiheit'. Anthroposophie und ihre Erkenntnismethode. Die christologische und kosmisch-menschheitliche Dimension der 'Philosophie der Freiheit'*, Verlag am Goetheanum, Dornach 2006.
51. Lecture of 20.10.1906. *Ursprungsimpulse der Geisteswissenschaft*, GA 96.
52. Lecture of 17.9.1909. *The Gospel of St Luke*, Rudolf Steiner Press, London 1988.
53. Lecture of 13.1.1924, *The Festivals and Their Meaning*, Rudolf Steiner Press, London 1996.
54. This explains why Rudolf Steiner called this capacity for devotion the chief teacher of the consciousness soul. See lecture of 28.10.1909 in *Transforming the Soul, Vol. 1*, Rudolf Steiner Press, Sussex 2005.
55. See *Knowledge of the Higher Worlds and its Attainment*, 'The Conditions for Esoteric Training'.
56. From the Constitution of the General Anthroposophical Society and the School of Spiritual Science.
57. For example in lecture of 28.9.1911 in *Esoteric Christianity and the Mission of Christian Rosenkreutz*, Rudolf Steiner Press, London 2000.
58. Lecture of 5.11.1911. *Esoteric Christianity and the Mission of Christian Rosenkreutz*, op. cit.
59. This does not mean that this is the *only* path to Rudolf Steiner.
60. Carl Unger: *Was ist Anthroposophy?*, Verlag am Goetheanum, Dornach 1996.
61. Lecture of 19.12.1915. *Die geistige Vereinigung der Menschheit durch den Christus-Impuls*, GA 165.
62. Lecture of 20.8.1923. *The Evolution of Consciousness*, Rudolf Steiner Press, London 1966.
63. Lecture of 18.10.1905. *The Foundations of Esotericism*, Rudolf Steiner Press, London 1982.
64. In his book *Knowledge of the Higher Worlds and its Attainment* Rudolf Steiner points to the importance for the spiritual pupil of 'develop[ing] within himself that all-embracing love which is necessary for the attainment of higher knowledge' ('The Conditions of Esoteric Training').

65. *Guardian of the Threshold*, Scene VI (*Four Mystery Dramas*, Rudolf Steiner Press, London 1998).
66. Lecture of 25.12.1923. *The Christmas Conference for the Foundation of the General Anthroposophical Society*, Anthroposophic Press, New York 1990.
67. See further in S.O. Prokofieff, *May Human Beings Hear It!, The Mystery of the Christmas Conference*, Temple Lodge Publishing, Sussex 2004.
68. Lecture held on 30 March 2006 at the Goetheanum in Dornach as part of the memorial service for Rudolf Steiner's death.
69. For more detail see S.O. Prokofieff, *May Human Beings Hear It!* (op. cit.), chapter 5.
70. Ibid.
71. See in more detail in S.O.Prokofieff, *May Human Beings Hear It!* (op. cit.), chapter 1.
72. *Autobiography*, chapter 30, SteinerBooks, Great Barrington 2006.
73. See H. Wiesberger *Aus dem Leben von Marie Steiner-von Sivers. Biographische Beiträge und eine Biographie*, Dornach 1956, page 28.
74. Later Rudolf Steiner took this law so seriously that at Christmas 1912, during the founding of the Anthroposophical Society, he not only did not join its Council but did not even become a member. I have discussed in another work the reasons why he later disregarded this occult law by becoming the leader of the General Anthroposophical Society. See note 3.
75. Letter dated 27 February 1925. *Correspondence and Documents 1901–1925*, Rudolf Steiner Press, London 1988.
76. *Marie Steiner-von Sivers im Zeugnis von Tatiana Kisseleff, Johanna Mücke, Walter Abendroth, Ernst von Schenk*, Basel 1984, page 55.
77. Letter dated 8 April 1904. *Correspondence and Documents*, op. cit.
78. H. Wiesberger: 'Marie Steiners Geistgestalt', *Nachrichtenblatt* 51–52/1998.
79. For more on the collaboration between some Freemasons and the Jesuits see lectures by Steiner of 4.4.1916 and 3.7.1920 (GAs 167 and 198—not translated).
80. J. E. Zeylmans van Emmichoven, *Who Was Ita Wegman?*, Mercury Press, New York 1995.
81. Ibid.
82. Ibid.
83. Ita Wegman already bore within her soul the capacities for assuming such a task, since she once participated in such a spiritual fight in the spiritual

world, where she had to take the leading role. (See lecture of 16.9.1924, *Karmic Relationships* Vol. IV, Rudolf Steiner Press, London 1965.)
84. Lecture of 22.2.1925, GA 36.
85. Albert Steffen, *In Memoriam Rudolf Steiner*, Anthroposophic Press, New York 1931.
86. See note 71.
87. Lecture of 21.10.1907-II (GA 101). Typescript Z 306, *White Magic Contrasted with Black* (Rudolf Steiner Library, London).
88. See: *Marie Savitch, Marie Steiner-von Sivers. Mitarbeiterin von Rudolf Steiner*, Dornach 1965.
89. Ibid.
90. From the letter to W. J. Stein of 9 January 1935. As quoted by J. E. Zeylmans van Emmichoven in *Who was Ita Wegman?* Op. cit.
91. Rudolf F. Gädeke *Die Gründer der Christengemeinschaft. Ein Schicksalsnetz*, Dornach 1992, page 31.
92. This individuality was not necessarily Edith Maryon, whom Rudolf Steiner called to be the leader of the Art Section during the Christmas Foundation Meeting (but not during the presentation of the Vorstand at the meeting), see *The Christmas Conference*, op. cit.
93. Of course this does not only affect the executive council in Dornach but every anthroposophical group that today looks for spiritual contact with and leadership through Rudolf Steiner.
94. See note 71.
95. For an earlier publication of this and the following essay, see Sources section, page 137.
96. Lecture of 11.10.1911. *From Jesus to Christ*, Rudolf Steiner Press, London 1991.
97. Lecture of 24.3.1908 (GA 102).
98. Lecture of 14.10.1911. *From Jesus to Christ*, op.cit.
99. *May Human Beings Hear it!* (op. cit.), chapter 9.
100. Lecture of 25.12.1923. *The Christmas Conference*, op. cit.
101. Lecture of 6.2.1917. *Cosmic and Human Metamorphosis*, Anthroposophical Publishing Co., London 1926.
102. Lecture of 26.12.1923. *The Christmas Conference*, op. cit.
103. Lecture of 1.1.1924. *The Christmas Conference*, op. cit.
104. Lecture of 28.9.1911. *Esoteric Christianity and the Mission of Christian Rosenkreutz*, op. cit.
105. *May Human Beings Hear It!* (op. cit), chapter 2.
106. 'The Portal of Initiation', scene 10, in *The Four Mystery Plays*, op. cit.

107. For more on the Foundation Stone meditation as summary of the whole of anthroposophy see S.O. Prokofieff: *The Foundation Stone Meditation, A Key to the Christian Mysteries*, chapter 1, Temple Lodge Publishing, Sussex 2006.
108. Lecture of 16.6.1923. *Die Geschichte und die Bedingungen der anthroposophischen Bewegung im Verhaltnis zur Anthroposophischen Gesellschaft*, GA 258.
109. Ibid, lecture of 17.6.1923.
110. Lecture of 18.11.1923. *Supersensible Man*, Anthroposophical Publishing Co., London 1961.
111. Lecture of 10.4.1914. *The Inner Nature of Man and Our Life Between Death and Rebirth*, Rudolf Steiner Press, Bristol 1994.
112. Lecture of 22.5.1905 (GA 93).
113. For more on the relationship between the heavenly Sophia and the Being Anthroposophia see S.O.Prokofieff, *The Heavenly Sophia and the Being Anthroposophia*, Temple Lodge Publishing, Sussex 2006.
114. Published in the *Nachrichtenblatt* 22/2006. See also Part I, *Nachrichtenblatt* 51–52/2005 and Part II 1–2/2006, Part IV *Nachrichtenblatt* 31–32/2006.
115. Lecture of 27.12.1918. *How Can Mankind Find the Christ Again*, Anthroposophic Press, New York 1984. In this lecture Rudolf Steiner uses the term 'real' or 'true' ego instead of 'higher' ego.
116. In the section in this book 'The Being Anthroposophia and the Christmas Foundation Meeting' (page 69) the Dutch Society was mentioned as representative of all other Societies.
117. Lecture of 27.12.1923. *The Christmas Conference*, op. cit.
118. Ibid., lecture of 31.12.1923.
119. *Karmic Relationships*, Vol. VI, op. cit.
120. S.O. Prokofieff *May Human Beings Hear it!* (op. cit.), chapter 6.
121. For more on the reverse cultus see lecture of 3.3.1923 in *Awakening to Community*, Anthroposophic Press, New York 1974; or, in the same work (German edition only, GA 257), footnote 46 of Appendix VII. In the lecture Rudolf Steiner speaks about the relationship of such working in groups with the *angel* beings.
122. Lectures of 18/19.10.1914. *Der Dornacher Bau als Wahrzeichen geschichtlichen Werdens und künstlerischer Umwandlungsimpulse* (GA 287).
123. *From the History and Contents of the First Section of the Esoteric School*, op. cit.
124. Christian Hitsch spoke of this in his lecture of 20 April 2003 (Easter Sunday) at the Goetheanum. See reproduction of his blackboard drawing on p. 78.

125. Lecture of 20.12.1917. *Bausteine zu einer Erkenntnis des Mysteriums von Golgatha: kosmische und menschliche Metamorphose* (GA 175).
126. Lecture of 26.10.1918 (GA 185). How important the development of this ability was for Rudolf Steiner, even within the newly founded Anthroposophical Society, can be seen from the letter to members of 18 May 1924 in *Die Konstitution der Allgemeinen Anthroposophischen Gesellschaft und der Freien Hochschule für Geisteswissenschft. Der Wiederaufbau des Goetheanum* (GA 260a).
127. Ibid.
128. Lecture of 17.6.1914, *Mysterienstotten des Mittelalters*.
129. Lecture of 22.4.1924 (GA 233a).
130. Lecture of 31.12.1923, *The Christmas Conference*, op. cit.
131. Ibid., lecture of 25.12.1923.
132. Lecture of 17.6.1923. *Die Geschichte und die Bedingungen der anthroposophischen Bewegung im Verhältnis zur Anthroposophischen Gesellschaft* (GA 258).
133. Lecture of 18.11.1923. *Supersensible Man* (op. cit.).
134. Lecture of 25.12.1923. *The Christmas Conference* (op. cit.).
135. *Die Konstitution der Allgemeinen Anthroposophischen Gesellschaft und der Freien Hochschule fur Geisteswissenschaft* (GA 260a).
136. 'Statutes of the Anthroposophical Society' in *The Life, Nature and Cultivation of Anthroposophy*, Rudolf Steiner Press, London 1989.
137. See S.O. Prokofieff, *The Heavenly Sophia and the Being Anthroposophia* (op. cit.).
138. Lecture of 18.11.1923, *Supersensible Man* (op. cit.). [This sentence is not translated in the English version.]
139. Ibid.
140. Lecture of 22.4.1924. *The Easter Festival Considered in Relation to the Mysteries*, Rudolf Steiner Press, London 1968.
141. Ibid.
142. Lecture of 1.1.1924. *The Christmas Conference* (op. cit.).
143. *The Influence of Spiritual Beings upon Man*, Anthroposophic Press, New York 1961.
144. *Anthroposophical Leading Thoughts*, Rudolf Steiner Press, London 1973.
145. Ibid.
146. Lecture of 13.1.1924, *The Festivals and Their Meaning*, op. cit.
147. Lecture of 19.7.1924, *Karmic Relationships*, Vol. VI, op. cit.
148. Ibid., lecture of 20.7.1924.
149. Lecture of 27.8.1924 in *Karmic Relationships*, Vol. IV, op. cit. These are

also those elemental beings who are mentioned in the Foundation Stone meditation as the ones who continuously call to anthroposophical souls: 'May human beings hear it'; that is to say, they want to remind us of what they were first taught in the Michael School. In the Michael imagination the elemental spirits are also called 'ether beings' of whom it is said:

Ye, the radiant beings of ether worlds,
Bear the Christ Word to man.

In the Foundation Stone meditation this 'Christ Word' is the threefold Rosicrucian verse.

150. Lecture of 25.1.1924. *Karmic Relationships*, Vol. VI (op. cit.). [This sentence has been omitted from the English translation.]
151. Ibid., lecture of 6.2.1924.
152. Lecture of 18.5.1913. *The Festivals and Their Meaning*, op. cit.
153. Ibid, lecture of 2.5.1913.
154. Ibid.
155. Lecture of 21.8.1924. *Karmic Relationships*, Vol. VIII, Rudolf Steiner Press, London 1975.
156. This can be understood as indicating that it still lies in humanity's future to work with the third hierarchy according to the new understanding of the Christ impulse based on anthroposophy.
157. Lecture of 21.8.1911. *Wonders of the World, Ordeals of the Soul, Revelations of the Spirit*, Rudolf Steiner Press, London 1963.
158. *The Spiritual Guidance of the Individual and Humanity*, chapter III, Anthroposophic Press, New York 1992, and lecture of 21.8.1911 in *Wonders of the World*, op. cit.
159. From what has been said it also follows that the esoteric structure of the Anthroposophical Society was formed in such a way that the impulse of the 5th post-Atlantean epoch can work at the level of the local groups, that of the 6th at the level of the national Societies, and that of the 7th at the level of the world Society. In our 5th epoch humanity generally has to learn to work with the angels; in the 6th epoch with the archangels and in the 7th epoch with the archai: a spiritual task for which an initial foundation has to be laid down in our time within the Anthroposophical Society.
160. *The Spiritual Guidance of the Individual and Humanity*, chapter III, op. cit.
161. Lecture of 2.5.1913, *Occult Science and Occult Development*, Rudolf Steiner Press, London 1983.

162. *The Spiritual Guidance of the Individual and Humanity*, chapter III, op. cit.
163. Lecture of 25.1.1910, *The Reappearance of Christ in the Etheric*, Anthroposophic Press, New York 1983.
164. Lecture of 21.9.1911, *Esoteric Christianity and the Mission of Christian Rosenkreutz*, op. cit.
165. Ibid., lecture of 4.11.1911.
166. See lecture of 6.7.1909, *The Gospel of St. John*, op. cit.
167. Lecture of 1.4.1913. *Das Leben zwischen dem Tode und der neuen Geburt im Verhältnis zu den kosmischen Tatsachen* (GA 141).
168. Lecture of 18.11.1911. *Esoteric Christianity and the Mission of Christian Rosenkreutz*, op. cit. On the relationship between the higher self and the true self see S.O. Prokofieff, *May Human Beings Hear It!*, chapter 4, 'The Foundation Stone Meditation in Eurythmy', and S.O. Prokofieff *Anthroposophie und 'Die Philosphie der Freiheit'. Anthroposohie und ihr Erkenntnismethode. Die kosmische-menschheitliche Dimension der 'Philosophie der Freiheit'*, Appendix I 'Über das Wesen des menschlichen Ich', op. cit.
169. *The Spiritual Guidance of the Individual and Humanity* (op. cit.), chapter III. What is said here corresponds to a note taken during answers to questions after the lecture of 23 March 1913: 'Physical body of Christ is the sun; etheric body of Christ are the seven planets; astral body of Christ is the zodiac; the ego of Christ still lies beyond.' (GA 150).
170. Ibid.
171. Lecture of 22.11.1919. *The Mission of the Archangel Michael*, Anthroposophic Press, New York 1961.
172. Ibid.
173. See 'The Michael-Christ Experience of Man' in *Anthroposophical Leading Thoughts*, op. cit.
174. Lecture of 9.11.1914. 'The Connection of Man with the Elemental World. Finland and the Kalevala'. Typescript Z 144 (Rudolf Steiner Library, London).
175. See GA 260a.
176. Ibid, lecture of 12.8.1924.
177. Rudolf Steiner uses this picture in his lecture of 17 December 1922. *Man and the World of Stars and the Spiritual Communion of Mankind*, Anthroposophic Press, New York 1982.
178. That the Anthroposophical Society really holds this task can be seen from the lecture in which Rudolf Steiner talks about these new group souls, and in this respect mentions that 'The Anthroposophical Society

is intended to be a first example of such a voluntary association...'
Lecture of 1.6.1908, *The Influence of Spiritual Beings upon Man*,
Anthroposophic Press, New York 1983.
179. Ibid., 1.6.1908.
180. It is not without significance that in the same lecture Rudolf Steiner also speaks about the 'intellectual, aesthetic and moral aspects' of humanity in connection with the effectiveness of the new group souls. According to his further comments the intellectual impulses are formed on the astral plane, the aesthetic impulses on lower devachan, and the moral impulses on higher devachan (see lecture of 4.11.1911, *Esoteric Christianity and the Mission of Christian Rosenkreutz*, op. cit.), which also correspond to the spiritual spheres of activity of the angels, archangels and archai.
181. *Occult Science, An Outline*, Rudolf Steiner Press, London 1979, p. 310.
182. Lecture of 1.6.1908, *The Influence of Spiritual Beings Upon Man*, op. cit.
183. Lecture of 15.6.1915. *Preparing for the Sixth Epoch*, Anthroposophic Press, New York 1957.
184. Lecture of 25.12.1923. *The Christmas Conference*, op. cit.
185. Rudolf Steiner speaks about this Michael love in *Anthroposophical Leading Thoughts* (op. cit.), chapter 9 'The World Thoughts in the Working of Michael and the Working of Ahriman'.
186. S.O. Prokofieff: *May Human Beings Hear it!*, op. cit., chapter 6.
187. Lecture of 25.12.1923. *The Christmas Conference*, op. cit.
188. Lecture of 1.6.1908, *The Influence of Spiritual Beings on Man*, op. cit.
189. Ibid.
190. Lecture of 7.9.1924. *The Book of Revelation and the Work of the Priest*, Rudolf Steiner Press, London 1998.
191. During the Christmas Foundation Meeting on 28 December 1923, Rudolf Steiner called the esoteric school the 'soul' of the Anthroposophical Society.
192. S.O. Prokofieff: *May Human Beings Hear It!*, op. cit., chapter 9.
193. Lecture of 24.8.1924, *Karmic Relationships* Vol. VIII, op. cit.
194. Lecture of 11.10.1911, *From Jesus to Christ*, op. cit.
195. *The Christmas Conference*, op. cit.
196. *World History in the Light of Anthroposophy*, Rudolf Steiner Press, London 1997.
197. Lecture of 1.1.1924. *The Christmas Conference*, op. cit.
198. See S. O. Prokofieff, *The Heavenly Sophia and the Being Anthroposophia*, op. cit.

199. *Anthroposophical Leading Thoughts*, op. cit., 'From Nature to Sub-Nature'.
200. *Perspektiven der Menschheitsentwicklung* (GA 204).
201. Ibid.
202. Ibid.
203. *The Karma of Untruthfulness*, Vol 1. Rudolf Steiner Press, London 1988.
204. The Revelation of St. John, 12: 3.
205. Lecture of 13.5.1921. *Perspektiven der Menschheitsentwicklung* (GA 204).
206. Lecture of 29.6.1908. *The Apocalypse of St. John*, Rudolf Steiner Press, London 1985.
207. The Revelation of St John, 13: 18.
208. Lecture of 19.7.1924. *Karmic Relationships* Vol. VI, op. cit.
209. For more on the special relationship between Sorat and ahrimanic spirits see lectures of 11/13.10.1918 in *Die Polarität von Dauer und Entwicklung im Menschenleben, Die kosmische Vorgeschichte der Menschheit* (GA 184).
210. Lecture of 19.7.1924. *Karmic Relationships* Vol. VI, op. cit.
211. Ibid.
212. Lecture of 21.9.1919. *The Mission of the Archangel Michael*, op. cit.
213. Ibid.
214. Ibid.
215. *Anthroposophical Leading Thoughts* (op. cit), 'From Nature to Sub-Nature'.
216. Lecture of 20.7.1924. *Karmic Relationships* Vol. VI, op. cit..
217. Lecture of 8.8.1924. *Karmic Relationships* Vol. III, Rudolf Steiner Press, London 1977.
218. Lecture of 13.5.1921. *Perspektiven der Menschheitsentwicklung* (GA 204).
219. Ibid.
220. Lecture of 20.1.1924. *The Christmas Conference*, op. cit.
221. Conversation with Mrs Sybell-Petersen (see appendix 2).
222. *Anthroposophical Leading Thoughts* (op. cit.), 'At the Dawn of the Michael Age'.
223. Lecture of 29.1.1911. *Esoteric Christianity and the Mission of Christian Rosenkreutz*, op. cit.
224. Ibid.
225. Ibid.
226. Science has already discovered that the human organism produces the same hormones during some computer games as are otherwise only produced by certain drugs. More on this subject can be found in the

book by Heinz Buddemeier, *Medien und Gewalt*, Menon Verlag 2006, and other books by him.
227. *Anthroposophical Leading Thoughts*, op. cit., 'At the Dawn of the Michael Age'.
228. Ibid., 'The Freedom of Man and the Age of Michael'.
229. Ibid., no. 105.
230. Ibid., 'From Nature to Sub-Nature'.
231. Lecture of 20.10.1906. *Original Impulses for the Science of the Spirit*, op. cit.
232. *Anweisungen für eine esoterische Schulung* (GA 245). (Extracts from this volume translated as *Guidance in Esoteric Training*, Rudolf Steiner Press, London 1972.)
233. *Anthroposophical Leading Thoughts* (op. cit.), no. 78.
234. *Michaelmas and the Soul Forces of Man* (op. cit.).
235. *Anthroposophical Leading Thoughts* (op. cit.), 'The Way of Michael, and What Precedes It'.
236. S.O. Prokofieff: *May Human Beings Hear It!*, op. cit., chapter 1.
237. Lecture of 22.4.1924. *The Easter Festival in the Evolution of the Mysteries*, Anthroposophic Press, New York 1988.
238. Goethe, *Wilhelm Meister's Apprenticeship*, Aegypan 2007.
239. Verbal comments by Rudolf Steiner to Frau Sybell-Petersen, communicated by Adelheid Petersen in a lecture in August 1950.

Sources of texts

The following chapters were first published in anthroposophical publications:

- 'Trust Born of Freedom': *Das Goetheanum*, 1/2004.
- 'Three Paths to Anthroposophy', *Das Goetheanum*, 12/2004.
- 'The Mystery Secrets of Rudolf Steiner's Birthplace', *Nachrichtenblatt* 8/2006; 11/2006.
- 'A Path to Rudolf Steiner', *Anthroposophie. Mitteilungen aus der anthroposophischen Arbeit in Deutschland*, 1/2006, Nr. 235.

- 'The Mystery of the Laying of the Foundation Stone':
- Part I 'The Laying of the Foundation Stone in 1923 as Mystery Event', *Nachrichtenblatt*, 51–52/2005.
- Part II 'The New Community', *Nachrichtenblatt* 1–2/2006.
- Part III 'The Spirit of the Goetheanum', *Nachrichtenblatt* /2006.
- Part IV 'Working with the New Group Souls', *Nachrichtenblatt* /2006.
- 'The Christmas Foundation Meeting and the Mystery of the Resurrection', *Nachrichtenblatt* 51/2004.
- 'Esoteric Background to Electronic Media', *Nachrichtenblatt* 44/2004, excluding the final chapter.